RUTH E. VAN

Letters Never Sent

"LETTERS" • INDIANAPOLIS, IN

Published by
"Letters"
P.O. Box 90084
Indianapolis, IN 46290-0084
317-251-4933

Distributed in Australia by:
Harvest Christian Products
P.O. Box 108
Upper Mount Gravatt
Queensland 4122

Distributed in New Zealand by:
GPH Society Limited
P.O. Box 74
Palmerston North
06-358-8180

LETTERS NEVER SENT
© 1988 by Ruth Van Reken

Edited by LoraBeth Norton
Cover © 1988 Comstock, Inc.
Cover & Book Design by Russ Peterson

First Printing, 1988 by David C. Cook
Printed in the United States of America

Second Printing, 1991 by "Letters"
Third Printing, 1995 by "Letters"
Originally published in 1986 as "Letters I Never Wrote"

Van Reken, Ruth
Letters Never Sent.
1. Van Reken, Ruth — Correspondence.
2. Christians — Correspondence.
3. Children of missionaries — Correspondence.
4. Nurses — Correspondence.
I. Title.
BR1725.V25A3   1988   209'.2'4   [B]   88-577
ISBN 0-9646423-0-1

CONTENTS

*To my parents
and three special MKs
Sheri, Rachel and Stephanie.
I love you all!*

A SPECIAL WORD ABOUT TCKS (THIRD CULTURE KIDS)*

by David C. Pollock
Director
Interaction, Inc.

A few years ago a forty year old "missionary kid," now involved in a productive ministry, listened to a presentation of a profile of a Third Culture Kid (TCK). By his own admission, for the first time he was able to understand why he felt and acted in certain ways. With tears he asked, "Where were people to help me twenty years ago?" My inward response to his question was, "We can't answer for twenty years ago, but by God's grace no TCK will have to ask that question twenty years from now."

Ruth Van Reken's "autobiography by epistle" is a contribution to the answer for every Third Culture Kid, be they MKs (missionary kids, BKs (business kids), diplomatic corp kids or military kids, in their process of development and adjustment. It is the story of one TCK's experience of conflict, growth, confusion and healing. It is the process of a life and thus must be read completely from beginning to end. Partial reading would be as unfair to the entire story as reading the Old Testament patriarch Joseph's life only as far as his prison experience.

As I, and others like me, have read the manuscript it has been with the awareness that it is not designed to condemn missions or missionaries, teachers, administrators or family. It is not designed to scream at the past. The book raises our awareness and sensitivity so that we may better obey our Lord's admonition to love one another (including TCKs) in the future. For those who have walked similar paths as Ruth, the account will be revealing and freeing.

All of us can be alerted to resist redoing history and instead improve our serving for the future.

This TCK is neither strange nor disadvantaged but rather a person with special experiences and opportunities which lend themselves to potential that must be developed and released. The TCK's needs are not different from those of anyone else. However, the demands and pressures of cross cultural involvement, high mobility, and highly motivated parents often create complexities in development that require unique insight and specific response. Ruth's story helps us gain that insight and develop our ability to seek proper answers to our own confusing questions as well as reaching out to others in their struggles.

*A Third Culture Kid (TCK) is an individual who, having spent a significant part of the developmental years in a culture other than the parents' culture, develops a sense of relationship to all of the cultures while not having full ownership in any. Elements from each culture are incorporated into the life experience, but the sense of belonging is in relationship to others of similar experience.

About The Letters
I Never Wrote . . .

This is a story about healing — not physical healing, but emotional. It took me a long time to recognize that I needed this healing; after all, compared to many other lives around me, my life was unquestionably good.

From my earliest days, I was taught of God's love for me, and I returned it. My parents' love was consistent. Their warm relationship to one another was a positive example. Despite the usual squabbles among my brothers and sisters, we maintained a deep commitment to each other. My husband, David, is a wonderful, loving man and an exemplary father to our three healthy, beautiful daughters. We had enjoyed our lives together, both in the States and overseas.

With all of this going for me, how could I be anything but gloriously happy? Yet under the appearance of perfection hid a person given to depression, anger, and a spirit of criticism. No amount of praying made it better. Sometimes things improved for a while, but soon everything was as before.

I couldn't understand why my soul, earnestly crying out for help, was unable to change. What was the key? Didn't the words I shared so glibly with others about our hope in God apply to me? Was I a total misfit? Why couldn't I be "victorious," when I had so many blessings?

After years of struggle, I crashed. I no longer had the strength to wrestle anymore. All I could do was run to God and say, "Here I am. I'm not making it. I don't understand how everything can be so good on the outside and so wrong inside, but I know I can't fix it. I've tried and tried. If You don't show me a way out, I'm lost. I give up."

Somehow the everlasting arms of God came and picked me up. "Ruth, I've been waiting for you to stop struggling so you can be quiet and see what I want to show you. Many of your symptoms come from hurts buried long ago. Everyone alive has hidden griefs — ones unrecognized even to themselves. Let me take you back so you can see just what yours are.

"You don't have to live the rest of your life in bondage to these painful experiences. I've promised that the truth will set you free, and that's not just the truth that I died for you: it's all truth, including the truth of your emotions.

"Don't be afraid to hold my hand and face all of your past. Yes, there will be tears as you remember some events. Opening up old wounds can be painful. But you can trust Me. I'll be as gentle as possible. I want you healed."

These letters are the result of my journey. Holding on to Christ's hand, I re-experienced — or perhaps allowed myself to experience fully for the first time — the lifetime of feelings I'd previously denied and put down on paper the letters I never wrote . . . .

RUTH VAN REKEN

1

OFF TO BOARDING SCHOOL

*M y story begins in Nigeria in 1951. Going to board-
ing school was a rite of passage for missionary
kids—a sign that we were growing up. Personally, I was
eager for the adventure to begin.*

*But right from the start, things were harder than I
expected. . . .*

SEPTEMBER, 1951

Dear Mom and Dad,

I feel awful. Something inside is squeezing me so bad I can
hardly breathe.

You said it would be fun to get on the plane and go to
boarding school, but so far it isn't. I couldn't stop crying on
the airplane, but I didn't want the other kids to know. I kept
my face to the window, so they might think I liked watching
the clouds.

When I got to school this afternoon, I was still crying and
I just couldn't stop. The missionary "aunties" who met us said

I should be more like Mae Beth. "Try to be big and brave like your sister," they said. "She's not crying."

They don't know that Mae Beth never cries. Not even when Spotty got run over by the car or our pet bird died. How can I be like her?

And how can I live without you? It feels like my heart got pulled out of me today.

Love,
Ruth Ellen

Dear Mom and Dad,

There is one thing I think you'll be glad to know—I didn't suck my fingers when I went to sleep last night!

The kids say if the teachers catch you sucking your fingers, they'll tie a sock on your hand for a week. You have to keep it on all the time, even in class, and everyone laughs at you. I don't know if that's true or not, but it sure scared me. I didn't know how I could stop, because I haven't been able to all the times you've tried to make me. I finally decided to put my pillow by my feet, instead of under my head, so I couldn't rub my other hand under it like I always do. Then it wouldn't feel so cozy to suck my fingers either.

When Aunt Gert, our housemother, came by, she asked if I wanted the pillow, and I said I never use one. It was pretty hard to sleep without you or my pillow.

I want my mommy and daddy.

Love,
Ruth Ellen

Dear Mom and Dad,

I'm scared to death. I know I'm supposed to obey the rules, but there are lots more here than at home. I'm afraid I'm going to do something bad and get punished.

One of the worst rules is you can't get up to go to the bathroom during rest hour. I don't know why, but as soon as I lie down every day for my nap, I have to go. I've tried everything, but nothing helps. I drink only the tiniest bit of water or milk at lunch, but the minute I climb into bed for rest hour, I have to go. By the time the hour is over, it really hurts bad.

Yesterday I did a naughty thing. I thought I'd wet my bed for sure if I had to wait the last half hour, so instead, I used my wastebasket. I forgot I'd done it until I emptied the trash after school. Some spilled on me when I turned the waste basket upside down!

I hope nobody finds out. I hate the idea that anybody besides you can punish me.

Love,
Ruth Ellen

OCTOBER, 1951

Dear Mom and Dad,
This is one day I wish I could forget. You know my boyfriend, Sam. (Did you know we were planning to get married and have twenty children? Only I think he doesn't like me anymore, because when we held hands the first day here, like at home, the kids laughed at us. They said we were in love. Since then we've hardly said a word to each other.)

Anyway, Sam is having trouble getting his schoolwork done. Today we were working on our reading workbooks. If we didn't finish in time, we'd have to stay in for recess.

Sam didn't understand what to do, so I tried to whisper across the table to him. (Even if he doesn't want to marry me anymore, I still feel sad to see him so scared about missing recess.)

The teacher caught us whispering. She said since we were talking when we weren't supposed to, she would have to tape our mouths shut. Then she made an X over each of our mouths with the tape. I put my head down on my arms on the table so everyone wouldn't see me cry.

It was even worse when she took the tape off. It left big white marks on our skin. At lunch the whole school was laughing at us because we were bad.

Mom, would you ever tape my mouth shut?

Love,
Ruth Ellen

Dear Mom and Dad,
The days aren't so bad now. After school my friends and I play Red Rover and Annie, Annie, Over. We also play jacks and skip rope lots of different ways. On Saturdays we go swimming in the dam and have a picnic in the evening. I can really swing high on the swings now, too.
But I hate the nights.
Every night I still cry myself to sleep. If my roommates hear me, they call me a cry baby. Other times they call the auntie on duty. She tries hard to cheer me up by telling me how much fun we're going to have at the picnic Saturday or on the walk Sunday.
I just keep wondering what's wrong with me. Why can't I get over missing you the way the other kids seem to do? Maybe I'm the weirdest person ever made, but I miss my house, my bed, my brothers, my parents, and my African friends at home.
I've learned to cry more quietly. But I've got awful snotty corners on my sheets, where I blow my nose at night.

Love,
Ruth Ellen

As I watched the other children apparently coping well, I concluded that the problem must be mine. But whom could I talk to? I was praised for my bravery and independence. If people liked my brave side, I reasoned, they obviously wouldn't like my frightened, lonely side. So the wall of "good adjustment" began to grow around my true feelings, and soon I was a captive within those walls.

Dear Mom and Dad,

I'm trying very hard to be good. I know everyone wants me to be happy here, and it seems like I should be.

Aunt Gert tries real hard to be kind and do special things for us. Lots of evenings we go into her living room, and it's a real cozy feeling while she reads us a bedtime story. I like to play with Tessa, the school dog. I have lots of friends, and there are lots of fun things to do here. When I'm doing them, I feel okay and I think that outside I look pretty happy. But way deep inside, there's some kind of sadness that won't go away.

There's no way I can write you about everything that goes on. For one thing, I can't spell too well, and some things take pretty big words to tell. Another thing is that it's hard to explain what I'm feeling.

The teachers try to help us write you by letting us a copy a letter off the board on Sundays.

> *Dear Mom and Dad,*
> *How are you? I am fine. This week we went (swimming, hiking, picnicking). It was lots of fun.*
> > *Love,*
> > *Name*

It's better than nothing, but if I were home I could tell you so much more. Printing takes a long time. Sometimes I see that the teachers write extra notes on our letters to you. They always say we're doing fine.

I suppose it's true, but I wonder how they know. Nobody can know another person's insides, can she?

> Love,
> Ruth Ellen

Dear Mom and Dad,

I don't cry at bedtime so much anymore. The teachers think I'm better adjusted—they don't know I've just given up.

Saturday nights are still really hard, because I think of you all going to the open-air meeting in town. I always loved that so much, and when I picture you there without me, I start to cry.

When I have to cry now, I just find some place alone. The others don't like to see me looking unhappy. I know they try real hard to make this school nice for us, but nothing is like your own mommy and daddy and home.

Love,
Ruth Ellen

NOVEMBER, 1951

Dear Mom and Dad,

I had my first spanking at school today. I had shown my music teacher my first wiggly tooth. It was fun wiggling it back and forth with my tongue when I was bored—kind of my own special secret. I wish I could have shown it to you.

Anyway, in music class, the teacher suddenly called me to the front of the room and said she was going to pull out my tooth. She's done that for lots of other kids, and they always seemed brave and proud. But, Mom, I was scared. I remembered the dentist pulling out four teeth when I was four years old. He had to put me to sleep.

I just couldn't let her do it. She said she'd spank me if I didn't let her, but I still couldn't. Mom, I'm sorry I disobeyed. But if they tell you I was a bad girl, I want you to know I didn't mean to be.

She spanked me and stood me in the corner facing the wall. I was so ashamed to be spanked in front of all those kids. I've never cried so hard in my life. At least standing in the corner helped hide my tears.

The class was singing "Oh, Susanna, don't you cry for me," and the teacher had them change the words to "Oh, Ruth Ellen, don't you cry for me." When the first and second grade went back to their room, and the third and fourth grade came in for music, the teacher said I was still crying too hard to go back. She made me stay in the corner while all those big kids were there.

I won't forget this day the rest of my life.

Love,
Ruth Ellen

Dear Mom and Dad,
I was in the infirmary for a few days. I don't like being sick when you're not here.

When I was eating supper there one night, I realized that my tooth was really loose. I shouldn't have been such a scaredy-cat about having it pulled. When I got back to school and saw my music teacher, I told her I was wrong, and she could pull the tooth. She got a tissue and it came out pretty fast. Now she's not mad at me anymore. I don't like it when a teacher is mad at me.

I wish there were a tooth fairy at school like there is at home.

Love,
Ruth Ellen

JANUARY, 1952

Dear Mom and Dad,
Thanks for a nice Christmas vacation. It was wonderful to see you again. There was so much I had waited to tell you, but when you asked me how school was, all I could say was "Fine." Why did I say that?

Maybe it was because I just wanted to forget about school while I was with you.

Maybe it was because I knew I didn't have a choice about going back, so there wasn't any point in telling you the truth.

Maybe I didn't want you to feel bad, since I know this is how we're serving Jesus as a family.

Maybe I was afraid you'd take the teacher's side and tell me why I shouldn't feel the way I do.

Or maybe it would take so long to tell you all that's inside of me that I don't know where to start.

I can't explain it. All I know is that the only thing I could ever say was "Fine." God knows it was a lie.

Love,
Ruth Ellen

MARCH, 1952

Dear Mom and Dad,

I'm excited that you're coming to spend your vacation near the school. I wish you could come more often, but I know it's far. And the teachers say it's not good for parents to come too much; they say it just gets the kids too upset.

I guess I see what they mean. By now, most of us don't cry as much as we used to. Everybody feels better about that. Maybe when you leave, it will hurt like before and I'll cry again.

Actually, I'm scared about your coming. When I close my eyes, I can't remember what you look like. What if I've changed so much that you don't recognize me? Will I know you when you walk by? What if we can't find each other?

I'm worrying about it a lot, but probably Aunt Gert knows you. If I ask her, she'll show me who you are.

I'm scared . . . but I'm counting the days.

Love,
Ruth Ellen

APRIL, 1952

Dear Mom and Dad,

Thanks for coming one day early to surprise us! Aunt Gert called us out of story time, saying there was someone waiting outside. She wouldn't say who it was. I didn't dare hope—but there you were with Chuck and Tom, and I knew you! You hadn't changed after all!

And you knew us, too. It's so great to be living together as a family for a while. I love coming home after school instead of going to the dorm. Now there aren't as many rules to keep. I'm still scared I'll forget one of them and do something bad without even meaning to.

Right now it feels like I have more room inside.

Love,
Ruth Ellen

MAY, 1952

Dear Mom and Dad,

I'm sorry your vacation lasted only a month. I was sad to see you go. At least summer vacation is coming soon.

I'm waiting to hear the schedule for the airplane rides home. Last time we were in the last group to leave. I wish they had enough planes to take us all on the first day. But if they send me home last, I hope they won't forget to send me *back* last, too.

I can't wait for the next few days to pass. Three whole months with you sounds like forever.

Love,
Ruth Ellen

2

THE SECOND YEAR

I couldn't understand the way I acted when I was with my parents that summer. I couldn't wait to get home for vacation, and at first I forgot all about school. Three months would never pass, so why worry about it? I loved being with my family again.

But about halfway through the summer, all the kids started thinking about the good things at school. They said they couldn't wait to get back again, and pretty soon that was all they talked about.

I saw the grown-ups smile at each other and shrug their shoulders. "See how much they like it," they all said. "They don't even miss us." They sounded relieved. I could tell they liked it better for us to say we liked school, rather than we missed home.

A few times I said, "I'd rather stay home than go back to school." But there was always some nice grown-up around who would say, "Of course you wouldn't. School is so much fun. I'm sure you'd rather go back, wouldn't you?"

*So pretty soon I joined the others in saying, "I can't
wait to go back." But when the minute came to leave,
all I wanted was to run back into my parents' arms.
Why did I say it, when I knew it wasn't true? It was
part of the wall, growing thicker all the time, that I was
building around my feelings. I couldn't let myself get too
close, when I knew I'd be leaving. It would only make
the pain worse.*

SEPTEMBER, 1952

Dear Mom and Dad,

I'm in Room 16 this year, in the new wing. It's neat, and
it's right next to the bathroom, too. Sometimes I sneak there
during rest hour.

I like having Barbie in the room across the hall. It's sort of
like we're still neighbors from home. I think it's hard for her
to be away for the first time, like it was for me. She looks real
sad.

I still cry, but not as much as last year. Maybe I'm more used
to it—or I know it doesn't do any good.

Love,
Ruth Ellen

Dear Mom and Dad,

Miss Crown is a great teacher. She's so gentle and kind. She
has such pretty handwriting, too. We're learning cursive, and
I hope I can write like her someday.

I write notes to Miss Crown on that little pad of paper you
gave me with all the different colored sheets. I slip the papers
into my workbooks when I pass them in. I hope she likes them.

Love,
Ruth Ellen

OCTOBER, 1952

Dear Mom and Dad,
Today another teacher came up to me on the playground and teased me about how much I love my new teacher. Then she recited the poem I had sent Miss Crown this morning!

I tried to pretend I hadn't written it. I wanted to run away and cry. Mom, why did Miss Crown show my notes to anybody else? I only wrote them to *her*. She must think they're silly and I am, too. I'll never send another note like that as long as I live.

Love,
Ruth Ellen

Dear Mom and Dad,
I have the mumps. I'm in the second group to get them, and we have to stay inside this one room so we won't spread them. They even bring us our food here. I feel like a prisoner.

Today Mae Beth came to the window to see how I was. She thought I was lucky to miss so much school. We decided that it would be fun if she had to join me, so I told her to come close to the window and I'd kiss her through the screen. We laughed and thought it was funny, but somebody reported us.

Later Aunt Gert came in and said we would just spread it through the school that way. That's why they're keeping us separate in the first place. I guess it wasn't such a smart thing to do.

I feel extra lonesome when I'm sick away from you. Nobody can take care of me like you do, Mom.

Love,
Ruth Ellen

NOVEMBER, 1952

Dear Mom and Dad,

Barbie is dead. I can't believe it. Why would Jesus take the nicest little girl here?

When she got sick a few days ago, we didn't think too much about it. Mumps are still going around. Then they took her to the hospital in Jos, and they told us all to pray. We did, but she still died.

At first I didn't feel too bad, because I knew God would bring her back to life. They keep teaching us about how Jesus did bring a girl back to life, and if you have faith a whole mountain will move. (I've been trying to move Mt. Sanderson behind the school that way, but so far I haven't seen any change.) Anyway, I really thought I had faith. I just knew God would raise Barbie. I prayed and prayed, and all through the funeral I waited for her to come out of the box. I wanted to run to her parents and tell them not to cry so hard, because everything was going to be all right. I kept thinking she was going to come back, even when they put the dirt over her. And back at school I kept watching for her, because I knew she'd be back soon.

The Bible says you can ask for anything if you believe, and it will happen. I can't believe that God didn't keep His word, but so far I don't think He did. Because I *really* believed.

Love,
Ruth Ellen

DECEMBER, 1952

Dear Mom and Dad,

I got your letter today, Mom, saying you hoped I'd act better during Christmas vacation than I did last summer.

I know I was too grouchy. Each time I come home, it feels

harder to let you hug me or hug you back. When I stay mad at everyone, it doesn't hurt so much to think about going back to school.

I'll try to do better this vacation, but I can't promise. I really do love you.

Love,
Ruth Ellen

JANUARY, 1953

Dear Mom and Dad,

I tried real hard to behave this last vacation. How did I do?

I found out that instead of getting angry and quiet all the time, I can pretend I don't care by being funny. When I joke about things at school or home, I can hide the hurt from you. I think you liked me better that way.

But either way, when the time comes to leave, I feel as though I lost something. I'm glad we're going to America next year. Maybe I can tell you more then.

Love,
Ruth Ellen

Dear Mom and Dad,

I'm confused. In devotions a few nights ago, Aunt Lucy said God can't hear somebody pray when he has sin in his heart. Well, then, I don't think I'm saved after all.

I asked Jesus into my heart after Sunday school when I was four-and-a-half years old. I had sin then, because I wasn't a Christian. That means God didn't hear me. Now every night I first ask Him to forgive my sins at least ten times, one after another, hoping He might hear me once by accident. Because since I'm a sinner, how can He hear me ask to be forgiven? And if I'm not forgiven, how can I be saved? Anyway, just in case He heard and forgave me, I ask Him real quick to come into my heart. But I don't know if He has or hasn't.

I wish you were here so I could ask you to explain it better. It makes me afraid.

Love,
Ruth Ellen

FEBRUARY, 1953

Dear Mom and Dad,

I'm scared to get my tonsils out, but I'm glad, too, because Mom will fly up to be with me. Otherwise, we wouldn't see you till June.

I hope I don't die in the hospital like Barbie did.

Love,
Ruth Ellen

Dear Mom and Dad,

I'm sorry I was such a scaredy-cat for my surgery. I know you were embarrassed, Mom, when I cried from the shots and fought while they tried to put me to sleep. I thought they'd choke me to death when they held me down and put that awful mask on my face. Ether smells terrible. My mouth tastes terrible, too, now that I'm awake and spitting out blood.

It's really not fair to be a kid. People can do anything they want to you, just because they're bigger and stronger and know better. I wonder if they remember what it's like to be little.

It was especially unfair to do it on Valentine's Day. I couldn't even eat the cinnamon heart from the top of the cake.

Love,
Ruth Ellen

Dear Mom and Dad,

I wish you hadn't gone home so soon, Mom. I'm back at school, but my throat still doesn't feel good. The worst thing is my ears, especially when I eat. Sometimes it's so bad, I leave the dining table crying and ask for medicine. Yesterday they told me it couldn't hurt this long, so I'm not allowed to do that anymore.

I wish I were home; I think you would believe me. My ears really do hurt bad, but I don't tell them anymore. I just try to suck my food instead of chewing it.

I suppose since I'm obeying them, they think they were right and I was just pretending. Grown-ups always think they know everything.

Love,
Ruth Ellen

APRIL, 1953

Dear Mom and Dad,

Mail comes about three times a week here. The other kids are kind of jealous because Mae Beth and I always get a letter.

Today Uncle Quentin kept calling the names on the envelopes, and kids went up to get their letters as usual. I began to get worried because our names weren't called and weren't called. I could feel all the other kids hoping that, just this once, we wouldn't get mail. Finally he got to the end.

"Well, that's it," he said. Everyone started to tease us, and then Uncle Quentin said, "Oops, I see one more." The other kids groaned, because they all knew it was for us. Uncle Quentin had just been holding it for fun.

I know everyone's parents can't send mail as often as you can, but I was so proud going up to get that letter. The whole school could see how much my parents love me! Thanks for that. I'm glad you're my mom and dad. And I love you, too.

Love,
Ruth Ellen

3

A YEAR IN THE STATES

JUNE, 1953

Dear God,

One thing I like about being a missionary kid is the trips back and forth to America. You've made a big world, and it's fun to see a lot of it.

I liked the boat and train rides in Holland (the art museum was kind of boring—who's Rembrandt, anyway?). I especially like it that breakfast in the hotel dining room comes with the price of the room. Eating there makes me feel more like other people. I don't like it when I see everyone else going to little cafes and restaurants, while we sit on a bench with a bag of bread, ham, and cheese that we bought in a store.

I'm ashamed to tell you this, God, when I know I get to do lots of special things, but sometimes I wish we had a little more money.

Love,
Ruth Ellen

Dear God,
   Thanks for getting us safely to America.
   I was surprised when the lady met us in New York. She wore red lipstick and nail polish and even earrings! In Africa we could tell who was a Christian and who wasn't by whether or not they did those things. Are Your rules different here?

Love,
Ruth Ellen

SEPTEMBER, 1953

Dear God,
   Thanks for helping me today. You knew I was scared to start a new school, but everybody seemed nice.
   The kids thought it was neat that I was from Africa, but they sure asked a lot of dumb questions, like how many lions and tigers I've seen or killed! Nobody believes me when I say none. And they've never even heard of Nigeria—everyone thinks I mean Algeria or Siberia. Well, at least they're friendly.

Love,
Ruth Ellen

NOVEMBER, 1953

Dear God,
   I really wish someone hadn't given us that heavy pink underwear for winter. I know they think we'll freeze here without

it, because we're used to Africa, but I wish we could wear the same kind of underpants that everyone else does. Why will we freeze if they don't?

I get so embarrassed when we have to take off our leggings in the coat room. I try to keep the underpants hidden, but I can't because they reach all the way to the top of my knees.

All I want is to be like the other kids. Jesus, you were kind of poor, too. Did you ever feel like that?

Love,
Ruth Ellen

In gym class we wore shorts, and it was hard to pull my underpants high enough to be covered by the shorts. One day one of the legs had loose elastic. I kept hitching at it, until I had to run around the circle in a game—then the whole leg fell down to my knee.

DECEMBER, 1953

Dear God,

Why did you let that happen today? Everyone laughed when the leg of my underwear slipped, but I couldn't stop running or my team would have lost. The more I tried to keep it from showing, the more the other kids laughed.

I *told* you I hated that underwear, God. I'm so ashamed I could die.

Love,
Ruth Ellen

MARCH, 1954

Dear God,

I think Dad was a little disappointed in me tonight. After he finished preaching in church, he asked everyone who was willing to give his life completely to Jesus to stand up. I know he expected me to stand, because I had already stood up two months ago at a different meeting. Maybe he was checking to see if I really meant it.

Well, I did mean it then. But afterward, all my friends said that little kids aren't supposed to do that; only big people can make that decision. They thought I was just trying to show off. So I'm sorry. I really do love You and want to do anything You want me to do. Only I guess I'm too young to say so.

Please help my dad to be patient with me. One day I hope You'll let him know that my heart did say yes, even if I couldn't stand up tonight. Thanks.

Love,
Ruth Ellen

APRIL, 1954

Dear God,

Did my parents doubt for a second what my answer would be? I couldn't believe it when they asked if we would like to stay at home for school next term. The answer could only be yes! A thousand yeses!

I can't believe they're willing to teach us themselves, or that they even thought of it. I know of only one other family that tried it, but it only lasted a year for them. Everyone at boarding school, including me, said they were big babies and had to stay by their mommy. I suppose we were jealous. I know my friends will say the same about me. I don't like that, but it will be worth it to be with my family.

Do I want to stay home? Yes! Yes! Yes!

Love,
Ruth Ellen

4

THE STAY-HOME YEARS

From 1954 to 1958 my parents kept us at home with them on the mission station, and my mother taught us. They weren't being defiant or trying to prove anything to anyone. They just made the decision that seemed best for our family.

APRIL, 1958

Dear Mom and Dad,

These four years at home with you are a blur of happy memories. Mostly what I remember are simple things like eating three meals a day together as a family. (Though I didn't always like getting up so early to have breakfast together before you left to teach school, Dad.)

I was proud when the local newspaper told about white kids going to school with black kids. They didn't understand that we were all doing our individual lessons in the back of the classroom while Mom taught the Nigerian students, but that was okay. I liked doing things that weren't ordinary.

I loved being free to go where I wanted and do what I thought was fun (as long as you agreed!). I know a school needs lots of rules to keep a hundred kids organized, but I loved not having to conform to all those extra demands.

It was great to go to the eye hospital and watch surgery. Do you remember the day I put on my play nurse's cap, and the doctor let me squirt the medicine in the patient's eye after the surgery? Right then I knew for sure I'd go into medicine.

Thanks for letting me go to the villages on Sundays with the language students. To see smallpox firsthand and to see the toddler who burned his head when he rolled into the fire were things I never could have experienced away at school.

My only uncomfortable memories are of going on vacation near the boarding school. I always felt that the kids were mocking us because we didn't go there. They teased me about my ugly hair and told in-jokes to let me know I was an outsider.

When the other kids from our station came home for vacation, they went on and on about how great boarding school was. Sometimes I thought maybe I was just a big baby for preferring to stay home. Once in a while I even felt sorry about some things they did that we couldn't, like having field days. But I never, not even for a minute, wanted to change.

I don't know if the other missionaries understood why you kept us with you. Maybe you've been criticized for it more than I know, but it doesn't matter. What matters is that we've had four years of family life that we wouldn't have if you hadn't dared to do what seemed right to you. Thank you, thank you, for keeping us all together. I do love you.

Love,
Ruth Ellen

MAY, 1958

Dear Mom and Dad

Today we're leaving Africa. I'm glad we'll be together for a year of furlough, but it's unbearable to think that I may never again see my home or closest friends or the country that I love so much. It's sort of like death—to lose your whole world in one moment.

Of course, it will be nice to see Grandma again. But, really, I know the people here better than I know her; after all, I haven't seen her for four years. I've lived here eleven of my thirteen years. Now, just like that, I'm expected to leave it forever and go "home."

What is home? A house? A country? A feeling? Sometimes I wonder if my strong desire to be a missionary is really God's call or just my way to cope with leaving. I only know that my small hope of returning is the only thing that dulls my pain today.

Love,
Ruth Ellen

JUNE, 1958

Dear Mom and Dad,

Thanks for being parents who live by principles instead of just rules.

You've always *said* that movies themselves aren't good or bad, it's what is shown in them. But we've never gone to any, for fear of offending other Christians who might feel different about it.

But today, when we asked to see the Walt Disney film here

on the ship, you said okay. There was no one to offend, and the movie was good!

I like it that you didn't change the reasons, just to make a rule stick. You make Christianity seem alive and real, instead of dead and buried.

Love,
Ruth Ellen

5

EIGHTH GRADE BLUES

SEPTEMBER, 1958

Dear Mom and Dad,

Was it hard for you to talk with your parents when you were thirteen? There are so many things I wish I could say to you, but even though the words race through my brain, they won't come out of my mouth. Sometimes I wish you could guess what's happening inside me.

You know how anxious I've been for eighth grade to start. My memories of third grade in this school are happy, so I figured it would be the same this time around. It's not. Instead of thinking it's neat to be from Africa, the other kids seem to think it's weird. I wore my very best outfit today, but it looked all wrong.

In the seventh grade there's another girl, Roxanne, who just came back from another African country. She really looks out of it; her hair is pulled straight back in a ponytail, and her clothes are very plain and don't fit well. I'm sure I'm not as bad as that (am I?). She wants so bad to be friendly, but the kids act like she's directly from outer space.

It wasn't a very good day—it felt like icy fingers squeezing around the pit of my stomach. I just don't understand the rules of the game. Hope it gets better.

Love,
Ruth Ellen

OCTOBER, 1958

Dear Mom and Dad,

The kids here think I'm incredibly dumb. Every day I do something that makes them laugh at me.

I make mistakes like saying, "Who's that?" when they mention a name, only to learn that he's the latest rock and roll star. I said something about a cartoon I'd seen on TV, and everyone was horrified. I guess eighth graders don't watch cartoons anymore.

If I talk about what I know from Africa or Europe, they think I'm showing off. No one is interested in my world, and I don't know anything about theirs. Why can't I go back to Africa, where I fit?

Love,
Ruth Ellen

NOVEMBER, 1958

Dear Mom and Dad,

I'm beginning to realize how hopelessly ugly I am. Here I am wearing nice, sturdy saddle shoes, and the other girls wear white gym shoes. My skirts are mostly cotton, but theirs are wool and corduroy. I've got lots of short-sleeved cotton blouses; they wear beautiful sweaters.

When I do get to buy something, I don't think I have very good taste. I thought my "wingy" metal glasses frames were pretty when I got them, but now I know they're too much. And there's no way to change them for years.

My teeth are crooked, too. When I smile, the kids think my front two teeth are knocked out. The teacher suggested that I get braces, but I'm sure we can't afford that any more than we can afford fancy clothes.

I've also gotten fat. It's nice of people to serve us all the wonderful goodies we haven't had for years: Hawaiian Punch, potato chips, ice cream, pretzels. They all taste terrific—but I'm thirty pounds heavier than I was when we arrived last summer.

What a basket case I've turned out to be. I guess I'll just have to accept that I'll never be popular or pretty, as I once dreamed of being. Maybe I can at least make good grades.

I know I shouldn't ask for more when my needs are being met. God was good to put it on someone's heart to buy me the shoes. The clothes cover me. My glasses help me see.

I know I have way more than most of my African friends—but it's way less than all the kids around me here have. In Africa we seemed rich. Here I feel hopelessly poor.

Love,
Ruth Ellen

DECEMBER, 1958

Dear Mom and Dad,

I know you don't understand what's happened to your nice, sweet missionary kid. I sit with my ear to the radio, listening to the latest rock and roll hits. Every afternoon I'm glued to the TV, watching Chicago Bandstand. When you ask, I say I like the music.

The truth is that I can't stand to be so odd anymore. I have to find out what's going on in this world, so I'll know what the kids at school are talking about. Yesterday for the first time I joined in one of their usual conversations about their favorite singers and songs. I think they were surprised that I had anything to say! It felt good.

I know you don't like my music . . . but thanks for not making me hide it from you.

Love,
Ruth Ellen

APRIL, 1959

Dear Mom and Dad,

I'm going on a diet. With my eighth-grade graduation coming up, I don't want to be so fat walking down the aisle. Maybe if I start high school a little less ugly, the kids will like me better.

I know I'll never be pretty or thin or gorgeous like the Miss America contestants. I can't figure out how to do all those beautiful hairstyles—maybe my hair just doesn't go that way. And I know my clothes won't be as good as everyone else's. But I can start doing something by losing weight.

I suppose it's not very spiritual to wish I were pretty, but I can't help it. I doubt I'll ever get married, because I'm so ugly. None of the boys thinks I'm cute, that's for sure. Besides everything else, I'm taller than everyone in my class except Robert. They probably think giants grow in Africa.

Love,
Ruth Ellen

AUGUST, 1959

Dear Mom and Dad,

It's been a good summer. I found out for the first time that I can actually feel God's presence in my life. I've always known

He was there, and I've tried to pray regularly and read my Bible. But in vacation Bible school, we studied the book of James and had to memorize parts of it.

As I think about the verses through the day, suddenly it's as if everything has come alive! God has promised to give wisdom when I need it. He says the struggles in my life will produce patience and character in me. Maybe all the things I've been through this year are for some good after all!

Love,
Ruth Ellen

6

HIGH SCHOOL

SEPTEMBER, 1959

Dear Mom and Dad,

My first day of high school. They've put me in the accelerated classes, so at least my strange education in Africa hasn't held me back in that way.

I'm hoping that starting over in a new school, with 400 kids in the class instead of twenty, will give me a chance. When kids ask where I'm from, I say Chicago. If only the kids who know me from eighth grade won't spoil it by telling others I'm from Africa, it will be okay.

Love,
Ruth Ellen

As the time for my parents' return to Africa drew nearer, I began to withdraw from them again. My anger grew and then gave way to the familiar pain, so great there were no other emotions left under which to hide it. But when I tried to express that pain, I always bumped into the reasons for the pending separation, and that locked me up. It was God's will that my parents return to Africa, and how could I argue with God?

I sensed that my parents were hurting, too, more than they dared to show. Our private pains seemed to make it impossible for us to bear each other's.

Dear Mom and Dad,

I wish we didn't have to go to the hostel in Michigan when you leave. I want to stay with Grandma and finish at this school. But I know what you think—Grandma couldn't handle me because I get too sullen.

I'm remembering the pain of first grade all over again. I see the same thing coming at me like a steamroller, and I want to jump in front of it and scream, "Stop! Stop!" But there's not a thing in the world I can do to make it change its course. Even while I stand there screaming, it will surely flatten me.

My mind understands just fine. I know lots of other families are worse off than ours. They have parents who are divorced or don't love them or are even dead. Knowing that doesn't make me feel any better. When I try to talk about what I feel, I always bump into the reasons for it all, and that locks me up. Does it hurt you, too, more than you dare show?

I've never needed you more, or been less able to say so.

Love,
Ruth Ellen

OCTOBER, 1959

Dear Mom and Dad,

So far high school is going better than eighth grade. At least I have gym shoes and bobby socks like everyone else.

Today an older girl from church was kind and told me I was carrying my books the wrong way. They're supposed to be one on top of each other, instead of side by side. I can hardly reach to the bottom of the pile this way, but I'm glad she told me. I'm trying hard not to do anything that's out of it this year. I just didn't know that how you carried your books made a difference.

Only two more months before you go. I'm praying that God will change His mind about sending you back.

Love,
Ruth Ellen

Dear God,

You must have heard at least part of my prayers. I'm not sure I even believed there was any point in asking for changes, because everything was so set. But I never expected the answer to be anything as mundane as a Spanish class. When Mae Beth signed up for Spanish last year, You knew they didn't offer it in the school we were supposed to go to. Now we have to stay here for this first semester, anyway, so she can finish.

Maybe Grandma and Aunt Mae will agree to let us stay on if we're good. Please, God. I don't want anyone but my family in charge of me again.

Love,
Ruth Ellen

DECEMBER, 1959

Dear Mom and Dad,

I'm sorry I'm hurting you. I see the confusion in your eyes. Here you are, about to leave for four years, and I'm acting awful. I know you want these last days to be filled with happy memories.

It's as if I'm trying to talk myself into the idea that I'll be glad when you go. If everything you do annoys me, then I'm better off without you. And maybe you'll be glad to be rid of me, too.

The problem is that in protecting the future, I'm losing the present, but I don't know what else to do. The prospect of your leaving is like facing my execution date. I can't bear what's ahead, so I run from it in anger and sulkiness.

I'm so sorry.

Love,
Ruth Ellen

JANUARY, 1960

Dear Mom and Dad,

I can't imagine how they thought Mae Beth and I would be able to sing a duet for your farewell service at church tonight— or how we were stupid enough to agree to it. How can I sing, when I feel like I'm on a torture rack being pulled apart more every moment? I didn't know it was possible to hurt this much and still live.

I feel so alone. Where can I run to? I'm afraid anyone who sees how badly this hurts will think I'm being disloyal to you . . . or to God.

I can't go to you for comfort, because I know your own pain is great. I've seen the tears you pretend not to cry. If I throw myself into your arms and sob my heart out, it might keep you from going. And even though that's what I want, how could I ever bear the guilt of being the one who kept you from doing God's work? I've always vowed I wouldn't be one of "those kids," the kind that other missionaries talk about in whispers, with a sad shake of their heads. "So-and-so couldn't come back to the field because of their children." They must be pretty bad kids, I've always figured. I don't want anyone to say that about me or our family.

And I can't very well come to God with this because, in a way, I feel like it's all His fault.

I did appreciate the hymn you passed to me in church when I cried beside you, Mom.

Ye fearful saints, fresh courage take,
The clouds ye so much dread
Are big with mercy and shall break
With blessings on your head.

I can't imagine what blessings could come from all of this, but I'm holding to that hope. If only I could stop the clock at midnight tonight.

Love,
Ruth Ellen

Dear God,

They're gone. Absolutely, actually, and finally gone. How could You have let it happen?

I feel like I've just buried them. I can't believe they'll all be alive in four years. When they marched into the plane, it was as though they were marching out of my life. Mae Beth and I will be in college by next furlough. As of today, family life as we have known it is over forever.

I wish I could take back all these past weeks when I've been so bad. Please don't let them think that's how I really felt. Why did I do that? Oh, God, what on earth can I do to get them back? or to let them go? or to be in peace? It seems like too much even for You to handle.

Oh, God, it hurts. Did You feel like this when you were separated from your Son?

Love,
Ruth Ellen

Dear Mom and Dad,

Aunt Jennette stopped at a store on the way to her house after we left the airport. I bought a record, "Teen Angel." It's a very sad song about a teenaged boy who loses his girl friend. She goes into a car stuck on a railroad track to retrieve his class ring, but a train hits the car and kills her before she can get away. I played it and played it today, crying every time. It seems less shameful, somehow, to cry for someone else.

How can the world go on normally for everyone else, when it just stopped for me?

Love,
Ruth Ellen

Dear Mom and Dad,

Knowing that nothing can change your being gone or my being alone, I have to shut you out of my life. It's as if I have to consider you dead. There aren't phones we can use to keep in touch. Letters take too much time. I have to face life as it has to be lived now.

When the ache comes, I push it back down. In the past few days I've cried enough tears for all four years, and I refuse to cry anymore if I can help it. And the only way I can do that is to try not to think of you at all. If I start wondering where you are or what you're doing, I immediately push the thought away. Africa is a different world. I will not meditate on it or you again.

Love,
Ruth Ellen

My method for keeping the lid on the pot of my family's separation seemed to work. Occasionally, if I wasn't careful, the pain bubbled up and raised the lid enough to let some seep out. But I quickly pushed it down and piled lots of activities and studies on top to keep it closed.

Thinking about my parents stirred up the pot, bringing it perilously close to boiling over, so I tried not to do that. I didn't want to get burned.

APRIL, 1960

Dear Mom and Dad,

I'm sorry I haven't written in a while, when you write us so faithfully. I'm awfully busy with school and activities. When I stop them, especially to write to you, I start to feel things I'd rather forget.

Sorry. I know it hurts you not to hear from me.

Love,
Ruth Ellen

Grandma and Aunt Mae let us stay on with them, so we attended high school in Chicago. By anyone's standards, I had a very successful high school career. I worked hard at being a normal kid. I joined Bible club and lots of extracurricular activities at school. I even got braces to straighten my teeth!

I made National Honor Society and was ranked ninth out of 365 kids in my class. I was voted "Girl Most Likely to Succeed" by my classmates, and I received three scholarships for college. High school was a good, even wonderful, time in my life. But I still missed my mom and dad.

JUNE, 1963

Dear Mom and Dad,

Tonight I graduated from high school. You weren't there to hear me make my speech as class vice president. I almost felt bad about that, but I got my emotions under control pretty quickly. "No, it doesn't bother me. I'm used to it."

Living with Grandma and Aunt Mae made all the difference in the world. They faithfully represented you every time a parent should have been there. They were at my graduation tonight. They've always let me bring my friends home, just as you would have. I've grown spiritually and physically.

But sometimes I wonder about *our* relationship. When friends fuss about their parents, I feel smug in my heart. *My parents would never do that*, I think. But would you? You write how proud you are of me—but would you like me as much if you had to handle my rebelling against curfew hours or turning down my radio?

I worked hard to keep you proud of me, and you haven't had to come home on my account. But do we know each other anymore? Your letters have been as faithful as they were in my boarding school years. You always tell me what you do, and I tell you what I do—but we rarely talk about what we feel.

I tried a few times, writing about my first crushes that weren't reciprocated, or how some boy liked me but I didn't like him back. I appreciated your good letters in response, but when they came a month later, I hardly remembered what you were writing about. After a while, it didn't seem worth it to write about that sort of thing.

I'm not worried about recognizing you physically, as I was in first grade. But my question is really still the same: Will I know you?

Love,
Ruth Ellen

7

HAVING PARENTS AGAIN

SEPTEMBER, 1963

Dear Mom and Dad,

Here I am at college. How did I get to be so old?

It's nice here in the dorm, but I can't believe how homesick most of the freshmen are. They run to call their parents every other night, and all they talk about is how much they miss home. It seems so silly.

But once in a while I wonder which is stranger: to be all of eighteen and still missing Mom and Dad, or to be only eighteen and not feeling homesick at all.

Love,
Ruth Ellen

OCTOBER, 1963

Dear Mom and Dad,

In a few days you'll be here. I'm a bit scared. How will we relate?

When Chuck and Tom came during the term, it took us a while to get readjusted to each other. I'm not sure they were thrilled to have two older sisters for mothers.

Now I'll suddenly have six- and seven-year-old sisters, who were practically babies when I last saw them. What do I know about six- and seven-year-olds?

And what about you? Will you expect to tell me what to do again? I'm pretty independent now, you know, and I like it. How will it feel to have parents again?

Will you still like me? I'm not fourteen anymore. Will you like the way I look or will you be ashamed of me? Will you like my straight teeth? Will you come looking like "missionaries on furlough"? Will I be ashamed of you?

I can't imagine what it will be like, but I'm anxious to see you. I think.

> Love,
> Ruth Ellen

Dear Mom and Dad,

It was hard to wait for Sociology to end today. When I ran across the campus, there you were. My very own family, in flesh and blood.

"This is my mom and dad." People acknowledged the introductions as if they were commonplace, not knowing it was the first time in four years I'd been able to say those words.

You looked about the same, not even much older. I'm glad you're here, but it's going to take a little time to get used to having a family again.

> Love,
> Ruth Ellen

November, 1963

Dear Mom and Dad,

Thanks for including us in your discussion about whether to return for another term. It felt good to know that our needs and feelings still matter to you.

Outwardly the conversation was calm and matter of fact. We named all the perfectly logical, absolutely true reasons why it's probably God's will for you to go back to Africa. We acknowledged His provisions for us: Mae Beth and I have had a home, we've done well in school, we've stayed on track spiritually. We're now away from home, anyway.

But everything inside me was screaming, "No, no, no! It isn't fair, God. Our family has already given you twenty years. You've taken and taken from us; can't you let us quit now? We'll serve You in the States."

But I couldn't—or wouldn't—tell you what I was feeling so deeply. I was afraid if I told you, you'd think I was saying you can't go back. I do understand your call. I even agree with it—that's what makes me feel that I shouldn't mind it so much. If I love God, as I think I do, and this is His will, then shouldn't I be feeling happy?

When I came to God later with my anger and my pain, He showed me these verses from Matthew 10: "He that loveth father or mother more than me is not worthy of me: and he that loveth son or daughter more than me is not worthy of me. And he that taketh not his cross, and followeth after me, is not worthy of me. He that findeth his life shall lose it: and he that loseth his life for my sake shall find it" (vv. 37-39).

What could I say? There are times when God requires us to give up our rights to family for His Kingdom's sake. But he also says that He will then supply our needs a hundredfold in *this* life, as well as the life to come.

I guess He's kept that promise. He's provided a close, extended family to care for me, friends in abundance, a warm home. If you must go back again, I must trust God to continue to be faithful.

But I wish someone would acknowledge the pain of what

He is asking. Just once, I wish someone would give me a hug and say, "I understand. It's okay to say that the right thing to do hurts. Go ahead and cry." (But is it okay? I keep thinking that if I were just a little more spiritual, this wouldn't be such a big deal.)

If only I could find just one person who would understand my tears. I don't want anyone to judge you badly for leaving me, or to think I'm unspiritual or unwilling to let you go. I just want someone to let me cry without trying to cheer me up or explain all about everything I already know.

Love,
Ruth Ellen

MARCH, 1964

Dear Mom and Dad,

The unbelievable has happened. God seems to have disappeared.

All through high school I was a leader in our Bible study. I witnessed eagerly, prayed earnestly, defended the faith vigorously. Now I can't feel God anymore. Where did He go?

This is my first crisis of faith since Barbie died. Isn't it ironic that it should occur after leaving a secular school for a Christian one? All around me are the right words, but there's so much cynicism among the students. Now I wonder if I've only believed all these years because it's what I was taught, or if God is real. How will I know? Even Bible reading, formerly my source of comfort, is meaningless.

In high school I claimed the verse, "When my mother and father forsake me, then the Lord will take me up" (Psalm 27:10). If He has left me, too, there's no hope. But in the prayer room on our floor, I noticed a sign today from Job 23: " . . . I cannot see him: But he knoweth the way that I take." That's what I'm hanging on to right now—God knows where I am, even if I don't know where He is.

Love,
Ruth Ellen

APRIL, 1964

Dear Dad,

Thanks for the great weekend. When I came home with my new and latest theories on predestination vs. free will, I expected to blow you away. But instead of the negative reaction I'd anticipated, you listened. You didn't get nervous or threatened that I wasn't spouting the party line.

How calmly you replied, when I had finished, "Well, Ruth Ellen, that's very interesting. I think you'll find that on some issues there may never be an absolute answer all Christians agree on, but God will give you understanding that will satisfy your heart. Just realize that if another Christian doesn't come to the same conclusion, you can be gracious to his viewpoint, too. In heaven, we'll fully understand all these things."

I was amazed. You were telling me it was okay to think about my faith, not just parrot it. You were saying you trusted me to God to teach me the things I need to know. Thanks for giving me enough freedom to keep searching for what I need to make the faith my own, not inherited. I love you.

Love,
Ruth Ellen

JULY, 1964

Dear Mom and Dad,

Thanks for the family vacation to the World's Fair. As you said, it may be the last time we'll be together, just the eight of us. Next time you come home, perhaps one or more of us will be married. That's hard to imagine, but a lot can happen in four years.

I knew how much you wanted this to be a special time for us, when we first stopped at the Dairy Queen. Instead of buying four malts to split among us, you actually bought one apiece. Two dollars and forty cents just for malts. We were in shock in the back seat!

Thanks for planning good memories of family time.

Love,
Ruth Ellen

AUGUST, 1964

Dear Mom,

This summer has been a terribly confusing time. I had no idea dating could get so complicated. Why is it that the guy I don't like as well always likes me more than the guy I *do* like?

When John told me yesterday that he wasn't sure about us and wanted to free me to think about Paul and others (and I didn't want any such freedom!), I was devastated. I sobbed my eyes out and tried to make sense out of my scrambled brains, and by 2:00 a.m. was getting nowhere. Suddenly it occurred to me that you were right here under the same roof, not a month's postal service away.

Dare I try? What would happen? When I finally gathered my courage to wake you, you just opened your arms, held me, and let me cry, even though you didn't yet know what it was all about. I needed that so badly! And when I was finally able to explain, your answer was all I needed to clear the fog.

"Honey, if you're crying this much about John, then I think you had better not say yes to Paul yet."

How simple! I don't have to make a life choice today!

How can a mommy still kiss an "ow-y" and make it better, even when the child is almost nineteen?

Love,
Ruth Ellen

SEPTEMBER, 1964

Dear Mom and Dad,

Once again, the inevitable moment of good-byes approaches.

Mom, I don't understand your peace. You've wept all furlough at the thought of going back, but now you are calm. You say the peace is from God. You told Him you couldn't return unless He promised He'd take care of all your kids, and He's told you through His Word that you can safely leave us in His hands.

It seems like an awful lot to trust Him for, leaving four of us in these years of so much decision-making. You must have had a pretty clear word.

On the other hand, it's rather awesome to know we are that confident of the keeping power of God. It feels like a lot to live up to, but it also feels secure.

I have to return to my verses of last fall to remind me that even the love of family cannot stand in the way of God's call on our lives. One part of me accepts that as a cold, hard fact. Another part weeps that it must be so.

My old defenses are surfacing, too. Mentally I'm jumping over the separation and thinking about nursing school, which starts the same week that you leave. Since I can't change the inevitable, I almost wish you were already gone. Then I could get on with what I have to do here.

Love,
Ruth Ellen

8

BEGINNINGS AND MORE BEGINNINGS

By the time my parents left for Africa, I was feeling numb and removed. "Oh, yes, they're going again," I could say, but I wasn't thinking about four more years of separation. I didn't allow any fleeting feeling of sadness or grief to stay around long enough to be recognized. I went straight from the airport to nursing school, and mom and dad's departure hardly seemed real.

SEPTEMBER, 1964

Dear Mom and Dad,

I'm mad at a new friend here at nursing school. She's so homesick for her family—she cries for them, calls them all the time, and thinks she wants to quit school and go home. And it's only going to be three months until she sees them again! What does she know about homesickness?

I'm beginning to feel proud of how tough our family is. . . . Do you think there's a bit of sour grapes here?

Love,
Ruth Ellen

MARCH, 1965

Dear Mom and Dad,

As I've dealt with people in so many hard situations each day in the hospital, I've gradually realized that apart from God there is no meaning or purpose in life. I'm thankful that the deep sense of His presence is again with me. Life is very dry without it.

Maybe part of walking by faith is continuing to walk even when the feelings all seem to be gone? It's holding on to what you *know* is truth, in spite of changing feelings.

Love,
Ruth Ellen

SEPTEMBER, 1965

Dear Mom and Dad,

My first year of nursing school is over. My grades are good, and I've had positive clinical evaluations. I also have lots of friends, not to mention a few dates! But in spite of the outside appearances of success, I don't feel that way inside.

I keep driving myself to accomplish more. What am I trying to prove? Is it for me? for you? No matter what I achieve, it doesn't make me feel more secure. I spend a lot of effort trying to shape what others think of me. My teeth are straight, I have contact lenses, my clothes are in style—but if someone says I'm pretty, I think they're just being nice. Inside I'm still the missionary kid with the saddle shoes and the pink underwear.

Things still crop up that make me feel stupid and naive, like conversations about china and silver. I can't imagine paying fifty dollars for one place setting of dishes or ten dollars for a fork! But the others are so excited, and they want my approval. I paste on a smile and nod enthusiastically, but sometimes I can't help myself. I blurt out something like, "How could you want to buy something so expensive? Think how you'd feel if you broke a plate or lost a teaspoon!"

Everyone turns and stares at me in shock, as though I just dropped in from outer space. It's eighth grade all over again, when I admitted that I watched cartoons.

No one else here grew up with cement floors, non-flush toilet receptacles that were emptied every day by a trap door to the outside, or lizards running through their homes. Will the feeling that I come from a different world ever completely die?

Love,
Ruth Ellen

That Christmas, Mae Beth got engaged and planned to be married in June. In the spring Mom wrote that she planned to fly home for the wedding. Then my dad wrote and said he had put out a fleece to God about whether he should come, too. The fleece was that if one of us kids wrote and asked him to come, then he would. Since none of us had done that, he wouldn't be coming.

APRIL, 1966

Dear Mom and Dad,

The greatest shock of my life is that Mom is planning to come home for Mae Beth's wedding. I never knew something like this would be "spiritual enough" to spend God's money on.

But, Dad, the letter I got from you today made me feel sick. Because none of us wrote and asked, you won't be here. You wonder if we're even glad that Mom is coming.

How could you?! My first thought when I heard that Mom was coming was, "I wish Dad and Alice and Marj could come, too." But the possibility that you would even contemplate such extravagance never occurred to me. And even though I didn't blame you for it, the very hurt that you weren't coming kept me from writing.

Why didn't you just decide you wanted to come, assume we would want to see you, and buy a ticket? I'm angry at being made responsible for your decision. I don't like blaming God, either, but there's that same old problem. We pray for direction. We don't want to do anything outside of God's will. We trust His leading and accept apparent results.

So what can I say, except that I wish I had written and told you my thoughts. If I say it now, it's too late. You won't believe me.

                                                    Love,
                                                    Ruth Ellen

JUNE, 1966

Dear Mom,

I don't know how we could have pulled the wedding off without you. I figured it would be easy for Mae Beth and me, with Aunt Mae's and Grandma's help, of course. But I never realized how much work a wedding entails. You did an incredible amount of sewing, cooking, and note writing. I'd forgotten how efficient you are!

It was fun to work together. To laugh and talk as friends as well as mother and daughter while sewing hems. To do the ordinary things like grocery shopping.

I'm also glad you got to meet David, after hearing about him all year. Good thing I didn't choose too quickly two summers ago! Thanks for coming. I'm sorry you had to go back.

Love,
Ruth Ellen

APRIL, 1967

Dear Mom and Dad,

What a spring vacation. First, there was my engagement to Dave. Now, sixteen days later, Grandma has died.

Why does God always take those closest to me? I love Grandma so much, after living with her these last seven years. Couldn't she at least have seen me married? The finality of her going is still incomprehensible. I feel a lot like I did the day you first left me for four years.

Yet I learned today about the beauty of death in Jesus, as well. Aunt Mae, Chuck, Tom, and I were all with Grandma when she died in her room upstairs. She asked us to move her arms and legs, as she was losing feeling in them. She was like a clock winding down. Finally Aunt Mae said, "Mother, we'll see you in the morning."

Grandma said, "Yes. Praise the Lord," and she stopped breathing.

When we came back to her room after calling the undertaker, Grandma's face was transformed. The pain lines were gone, she looked at least thirty years younger, and there was a gentle smile on her face. I knew she had seen God or His angel come to take her home—the welcome was written all over her face.

I thought of all the patients in the hospital to whom I've helped give resuscitative measure when there really was no hope. This is a far better way—to accept God's call with grace, dignity, and joy. To go majestically, not reluctantly.

I have one thing to say to you about my life, Mom and Dad. There's been a lot of pain in it, but there's been an even greater amount of beauty.

Love,
Ruth Ellen

MAY, 1967

Dear Mom and Dad,
I had a rather odd experience with the Lord the other night. While I was reading the Bible, I came to Isaiah 61:1-3. It seemed the verses suddenly jumped out at me, and God was saying, "The Spirit of the Lord God is upon you, to bind up the brokenhearted, to comfort those that mourn," and all the rest those verses say.

I guess it fits with my being a nurse; after all, I take care of people daily who need physical binding up as well as emotional and spiritual. It was just startling how clear it all seemed, that this was my basic assignment for life. I wonder what it all means. Has anything like that ever happened to you?

Love,
Ruth Ellen

Dear Mom,
Another great shock! I just got your letter saying you're coming home now, instead of next year, to help Aunt Mae take care of Chuck and Tom. And Dad will also come, in time for my wedding this summer. I never thought you'd consider such a thing, or that you and Dad would separate for three months just for us.

I'm thrilled, of course. Just struggling with a little guilt that your children are keeping you from God's work.

Love,
Ruth Ellen

JULY, 1967

Dear Mom and Dad,

As my wedding day approaches, I'm getting more scared. I can't believe God will let me keep David. It's like He's dangling Dave on a rope, letting him come closer and closer. I'm afraid that at the last moment, when I put out my hand to take him, the string will be jerked back and God will laugh.

"Ha ha. Thought you finally had someone you could keep. Don't count on it. Whatever you depend on, I will surely take that, so that you'll depend solely on Me."

As much as I love David, inside there is a holding back. If I stay prepared for him to be taken, it won't hurt so much when it happens. And if I hold back, maybe God won't notice that I'm almost totally happy, and He'll let me keep Dave.

I know this is a terrible concept of God. I doubt it's a very healthy way to start a marriage, either. But that's what I'm feeling.

Love,
Ruth Ellen

AUGUST, 1967

Dear Dad,

I'm so glad you're finally here. Once more my heart is full of things I long to share with you. I wish I could sit on your lap and be your little girl again, and tell you all about my fears and dreams for the future.

But it's too late, Dad. The wall is still there. There isn't time to catch up on everything, and in three more days I'll belong to somebody else, not you. It seems safer not to get started.

Do you realize all the important things that have happened in the three years since I've seen you? My capping, choir concerts, the time I sang in a trio at McCormick Place, graduation, baccalaureate, Mae Beth's wedding. You missed every one.

I've chosen my life's partner while you were gone and you, my own father, have had no input except to respond to what I've written about him. I did appreciate the telegram you sent when I first met Dave, wondering if it was all happening too fast. The Scriptures you sent helped to keep me steady and walk a step at a time.

In a way it's an honor, Dad, that you believe enough in me, in how you raised me, and in God that you trust the decisions I've made. I know you will accept and love David just because I do. But it would have been nice to bring him home to *you*, instead of only to my aunt and brothers and sister.

How can he really know me without knowing you — everyone says I'm like you. To Dave, it's as though I have no connections. Can he truly understand who I am without understanding where I've come from? He might not realize the chance he's taking!

Even my name has changed now; though I've told Dave many times that I have a double name, to him I'm just plain Ruth or Ruthie. I always felt that it was the "Ellen" part of my name that made me distinctive from the all other Ruths in my classes . . . but I suppose Ruth Ellen Van Reken would be too long, anyway.

I feel sad that the two most important men in my life don't know each other at all.

Love,
Ruth

Dear Dad,

I heard you come into my room this morning. You stood there, probably thinking of the fact that this was my last morning as just your daughter and not someone else's wife.

I felt your love, and I wanted to open my eyes and respond, but something stopped me. I didn't know what I would say or do. I would have liked to tell you all the things I appreciate about you, but if I had let the wall down today, it might have made tonight's leaving unbearable. So I waited to see what would happen. Would you wake me and say something? Should I open my eyes and let you know I knew you were there?

My eyes stayed shut. You kissed my forehead and walked away, and the moment was lost forever. I'm sorry, Dad.

Love,
Ruth Ellen

9

WHERE'S MY PERFECT MARRIAGE?

SEPTEMBER, 1967

Dear Mom and Dad,

God didn't yank David away, after all! And I'm glad He didn't, for I love being David's wife. But the fears haven't left. I recently saw a book about a couple who had a car accident right after their wedding, and the wife was killed. Driving down to Tennessee for our honeymoon, I just knew it would happen to one of us. I can't get over the feeling that God won't allow me to keep anyone I love for very long.

We're having too nice a time, just doing what we want, when we want, enjoying each other's company. It's scary—it doesn't seem spiritual to have this much happiness with another person.

Love,
Ruth

FEBRUARY, 1968

Dear Mom and Dad,

We've been married for half a year already, and so far nothing too awful has happened. Of course, any time Dave is a few minutes late, I pass the time planning his funeral. I've even wondered how long you have to be married before you don't need to return the wedding gifts,. should something terrible happen.

I wish I could get over this fear. One thing that helps me believe that maybe God does actually love me enough to let me have something so wonderful is the absolute consistency of David's love. I think I often test it, just to see if he, too, won't leave me or give up. But he's always there, steady as a rock, continuing to love me even when I don't deserve it. I'm sure your love has been like that, too, but being away from you so long makes your love more of a memory than a daily operation.

I find it hard, though, even with David, not to put up a tiny wall. Not having any would leave me too vulnerable.

Love,
Ruth

AUGUST, 1968

Dear Mom and Dad,

Can you believe it's our first anniversary already? What a good year, what a hard year it has been.

The most difficult thing has been finding out that I'm not a perfect wife. I guess that shouldn't have been such a surprise— I wasn't ever a perfect roommate back in college or nursing school days—but somehow I expected marriage to be different. I thought I would blossom into the ideal wife I remember you to be, Mom. And I thought that Dave would be the perfect husband that I remember you as, Dad.

Is my memory faulty from all the years apart, or is your marriage truly an exception? The only time I remember your being cross with each other was on the trip to the New York World's Fair. Mom was reading the map, and we got lost. After you pulled to the side of the road, Dad, you snapped the map out of her hand and said, "Here. Let *me* see it." We kids just looked sideways at each other, because we'd never seen that happen before—and I was *eighteen years old* at the time!

A few years ago Aunt Jennette told me that when I got married I'd feel terrible the first time I had an argument with my husband. Although I heard her politely, in my heart I didn't believe that married people fought . . . at least I knew that I never would! My marriage would doubtless be as perfect as yours has been.

Each disagreement we have leaves me shattered, but Dave never seems to think it's anything big. I guess he's more used to living with the daily ins and outs of marriage in his home. And now I suppose that you must have had disagreements over the years . . . but I still can't imagine you having the kind of petty fights we have.

All my life I've thought I was pretty tough and able to be what I'd decided to be. You wrote me lovely letters on how to be a good wife, and I knew without a doubt that I would be. But I'm not. I can be lazy, selfish, tired, and crabby. Sometimes when Dave has to study, and I'd rather do something together for the evening, I get hurt feelings and am not at all understanding.

I feel like such a failure. Dave forgives me, but I can't forgive myself. Even though I've seen you several times this past year, I haven't been able to talk with you about this. It's bad enough to have my own image of myself destroyed, to say nothing of poor David's image of me. I'd like to leave yours intact. And you'll soon be leaving, anyway, so why should I bother you?

Love,
Ruth

My parents returned to Nigeria at the end of the summer. After they left, I found that I couldn't reconstruct the moment of their departure in my memory. I had absolutely no recollection of how, when, or from where they left. I was amazed at how well trained my pain-protecting mechanisms had become; from the total devastation of the first time they left me, I had come to this, a complete blocking out of their departure.

SEPTEMBER, 1968

Dear Mom and Dad,
    There's something else I wish I had talked to you about this past year: in-laws. Since Grandma Varnell was the only grandparent I knew, I never learned anything about in-law relations.
    Dave's folks may be the world's best in-laws. They're warm, giving people who would do anything in the world for us. They want us to live our own lives and try hard not to interfere. But I find that, after so many years of independence from parents, I resent normal parental interest.
    It's such small stuff—suggesting to Dave that a different tie might look better with his suit, seeing a button that needs to be tightened, offering to share a recipe, suggesting what kind of insurance is good or bad. Even his brothers wanting to play ball with him, when I'd rather do something else.
    I feel a tightening inside. I'm sure they can sense it, but they can't understand what is happening. How can they comprehend that I haven't had my own mom telling me what to wear since eighth grade, or that sewing buttons on has been solely my responsibility for nine years (except when I could con Grandma into doing them for me!). You weren't there to

ask lots of advice from, so I learned to make big decisions for myself. Now I don't know how to accept normal parenting, and I hate the resentment I feel.

Maybe what I really resent is that Dave's parents are here, while mine are nowhere in sight.

Love,
Ruth

JANUARY, 1970

Dear Mom and Dad,

Today we learned that we've received a Smith-Kline-French fellowship award to come and spend six months in Jos next year, when Dave is a senior in medical school. I can't believe it! Not only to see you, but to come home? It's a dream come true.

We're both slated to work in the hospital there, but I'm not sure how my schedule will work out, since we also learned this week that I'm expecting! The baby is due a month after we come. People will think I'm crazy to have my first baby in Africa, but I think it's terrific. I know one can have a baby quite safely out of the U.S. — you did it six times! And I'm so excited to think of your sharing such a special moment in my life. Alice and Marj will be instant aunts!

To think of seeing my old friends, my house, my country, everything, after all these years, and to be able to share it all with David. I don't think he's able to comprehend just how much my life in Africa has meant to me, but it's not his fault. How can you really explain to someone who hasn't been there what Africa is all about? You can't explain it — you can only experience it.

Love,
Ruth Ellen

*In the six months after getting our scholarship, our
visas for Nigeria never came through. I was sure that if
God provided the money, surely He would send the visas,
too. Visas were hard to get at the time, so I even wrote
the Nigerian government and asked them specially to let
us come, so that I could have my baby in the country
of my birth. We heard nothing, not even a refusal.*

AUGUST, 1970

Dear Mom and Dad,

Well, God's done it again. Why? Why? Does He just like to
be mean to me?

Until a couple weeks ago, I didn't face the possibility that
it might be God's will that we not come to see you. Then as
I prayed, it was as if His voice said, "Ruth, do you want to do
My will or yours?" I was shocked. Since I was a child, I've
always felt God's will was for me to go back. One of the reasons
I was so sure I should marry Dave was that he, too, had planned
for years to be a missionary doctor to Nigeria. I can even speak
the language. How could it possibly be anything but God's will
for us to go?

Finally I told the Lord that I have always wanted to do His
will, even it doesn't include Nigeria. I made a covenant with
Him that if the visas didn't come by August 1, I'd know we
should make other plans. The deadline has come and gone,
and we must do something with our fellowship. So I'm writing
to let you know we will be going to Liberia, instead.

Once again I realize that sometimes the greatest act of faith
is obedience, even when there aren't feelings to back it up.

Love,
Ruth

10

BACK TO AFRICA

*T*hough I was disappointed that we couldn't go to Nigeria, I was surprised to discover how familiar Liberia felt. When the plane landed in Dakar to refuel, I had to get out and just step on African soil—though my feet were so swollen I couldn't get my shoes on properly. Sitting up all night with an eight-month pregnancy in one's lap isn't great for the circulatory system!

As soon as I left the plane to walk down the steps, I knew I was home! Tropical sights and smells, the heat at such an early morning hour, people speaking an African dialect. Even the way the plane could land without circling for an hour first!

We were met in Monrovia by my mother's sister Lois and Uncle Ell and their kids. If we couldn't be with my parents, it was nice at least to be met by relatives.

SEPTEMBER, 1970

Dear Mom and Dad,

I wish my brothers and sisters could be with me. Would they, too, experience things long forgotten as instantly familiar once again? A little girl came by selling oranges yesterday, and I suddenly remembered, "Of course! Oranges are green in Africa!" I love watching the ease with which the women put babies on their backs, adjust the loads on their heads, and walk off.

I haven't felt this at home for the past twelve years in the States. And the greatest thing is seeing that Christianity is still alive, well, and practical. People here live in total dependence on God for all their needs. It's a challenge to my faith. At the first church service, I revelled in seeing so many skin colors, types of dress, and people from different nations, all participating in the remembrance of Christ by taking Communion together. In the six men serving the elements, five nationalities were represented! God seems big and alive once again.

I feel like a sponge, soaking up the riches of being back.

Love,
Ruth

OCTOBER, 1970

Dear Mom and Dad,

Sheri Lisa was born yesterday. What an experience. One minute so much pain and inner work, the next total peace and outer awareness. From nowhere comes this fantastic, marvelously formed *person!* Incredible!

I'm sorry that you weren't around as I had hoped, but it was great for Dave to be with me. Aunt Lois and Uncle Ell came to visit right away, and we had a wonderful time enjoying Sheri together.

The Liberian expression of congratulations is "Thank you

for the baby"! I'm not quite sure how to respond, but it makes me feel like I'm the first person who's ever had a baby in such a magnificent fashion, or ever had such a perfect one!

As I lie here watching my baby in the crib beside me, I am overwhelmed. I'm Sheri's mom, but I have no idea at all who she is. What's her personality? What are her gifts? Her weaknesses? Who *is* she? Although I don't know a thing about her, I feel such unbelievable love and protection toward her, just because she's mine. And with that great love comes great potential for pain.

I never knew before how I must have hurt you all those years, when I let months go by between letters. I didn't think it mattered. I guess I've taken your love pretty much for granted. How many tears did you cry that I never saw?

Love,
Ruth Ellen

On October 20th, we received a radio message saying that Mae Beth and her husband and three-month-old daughter had been in a head-on collision. Ken broke his kneecap. Mae Beth broke her arm and leg and suffered facial lacerations requiring over 200 stitches. Baby Kerrie, who went through the windshield in Mae Beth's arms, broke her collar bone. We were thankful that they all were alive.

Dear Mom and Dad,

It's terrible to be so far apart in a family crisis. Mae Beth has only her in-laws there to take care of her and help her care for Ken and Kerrie. Our side of the family should be physically present, too, not just to help but to say, "We love you, and we're so sorry." But here we sit again, thousands of miles apart. We know Mae Beth understands. We're all pretty good at rationalizing and accepting these inevitable moments, but why did it have to happen while I'm here?

In my mind I keep seeing Kerrie go through windshield in Mae Beth's arms, and I realize how easily they could have lost her. As I watch my own five-day-old baby, I'm obsessed with the old terror that God won't let me keep something I love so much. Why does the past continue to haunt me?

Love,
Ruth

DECEMBER, 1970

Dear Mom and Dad,

Today we got our visitors' visas, so we can come see you for three weeks over Christmas. Now I have mixed feelings. I want you to meet Sheri, and yet—it's been two and a half years since I saw you. I'm used to your absence again. If I see you now, my careful equilibrium will be upset once more. The old "whys" will return, and I'll have to endure the too-familiar pain of leaving one more time.

Why put myself through all that for just three weeks?

Love,
Ruth

JANUARY, 1971

Dear Mom and Dad,

I had no idea you would be such doting grandparents! I thought you'd accept it as almost routine, but there you were, making sure everyone was introduced to us *and* to Sheri! And, like any other grandparents I've ever seen, you kept your "brag book" handy for all interested or non-interested observers. I loved it!

It made me realize how you must have felt toward us when we were babies. Not that I ever doubted your love, but seeing you with Sheri gave me a new vision of it. You were as proud of us as we are of her!

Laced through the good times was the same old feeling of time being too short. My sisters have become young ladies. How did they grow so fast? As I watched you play with Sheri, I was sharply aware that you'll miss all the next stages of her life. You won't see her again until she's walking, maybe even talking.

Dave's family will see all the in-between stages. It's inevitable that she'll grow up knowing the Van Reken family far better than the Frame family. Of course, I want her to know them—I just wish so badly that she could know you as well.

Love,
Ruth Ellen

Dear Mom and Dad,

Oh, the memories revived by being back in Nigeria. Mostly they were good ones, but I felt some twinges of pain when we walked around the boarding school campus. Everyone said what a great place it was and how happy all the kids were. They certainly looked happy, playing on the swings and running about. I hoped they really were. But then I began to remember. . . . Outwardly, I'm sure that seven-year-old Ruth Ellen looked happy, too. Was it possible that any of the children we saw were missing their moms and dads as much as I did? Do they think they are the only ones who feel that way?

I know boarding school has changed, and parents can come to visit more often that they did in my school days. But I couldn't help wondering if there might be some child among all those I saw who felt like a failure because she'd secretly rather be with her mom and dad.

Love,
Ruth

Dear Dad,

Christmas Day was just as I remembered it. Stockings for everyone, even Sheri, and church in the morning. Presents to open and a great Christmas dinner. Even the old faithful tinfoil "Merry Christmas" sign on the wall!

The one hard moment came during the meal, when you were carving the turkey and Mom asked you to pass the gravy. With infinite forbearance, you replied, "I will, when I finish cutting the turkey. I can't do everything at once."

In that instant I realized how much like you I am. Dave will ask me where the salt is, when I've just sat down to eat. Instead of saying, "In the cupboard," I take a deep breath, grit my teeth, and go to get it. Then I remain in wounded silence the rest of the meal.

Dad, do you understand that in my memory all these years, you've been almost perfect? I suppose if someone pinned me down, I'd have said, "Well, of course no one is perfect—but my parents are pretty close." On Christmas Day I felt cheated. It was such a small thing, but you weren't perfect. How could you be a mortal like everyone else's dad?

All my life I've tried to live up to the image I have of you. Maybe I couldn't face my own imperfections honestly enough to admit to some of yours. But especially since I got married, I've been constantly reminded of how far short of perfect I fall. I'm realizing how many things I actually dislike about myself, and I want to blame you for all of them. We do act an awful lot alike.

Love,
Ruth

Dear Mom,

Thanks for listening when I told you my feelings about Dad and the turkey incident. I appreciated your sharing your own similar experience, when you came back from college your first Christmas vacation and saw your parents as people, not just parents. But then you said the good thing was that now I could see myself better and work on changing the things I don't like.

I know you're right, but I want to rebel. Don't you understand? It's a lot easier to let myself off the hook by blaming Dad, rather than take responsibility for my own behavior.

Love,
Ruth Ellen

Dear Mom and Dad,
Thanks for the trip up to Kano, so I could see the area where I grew up. It sure didn't look like my memories.

I thought we had such a big, pretty house; now I wonder how you ever raised six kids in that tiny place. We used to swim in that tub, but I don't think I could sit with my feet straight out in it now. The compound seemed so big to me then—I thought Carol's house was too far away unless I had my bike to ride. I doubt it's a city block away.

The trees used to be friendly and kind; now they're so big no one could climb them. I looked for the one Sam and I carved our initials on, but I couldn't find any sign. So many buildings have gone up in the surrounding area. I didn't like my memories being tampered with, even by "progress." And I resented the fact that someone had painted over the nice wooden bookcases Dad built into our living room walls. They look cheap and silly now.

The all-too-familiar part of the trip was when the car broke down. But, now as then, Dad improvised, making a fan belt out of palm leaves, and we limped along until we found help. Your great resourcefulness always got us through somehow. It wouldn't have been an authentic trip without such an incident!

Thanks again for making the trip possible, but I didn't like the changes. I think I'll go back to remembering Kano the way it was.

Love,
Ruth

Dear Mom and Dad,

When the dreaded moment of leaving came, I did what I had expected to do—I cried. Dave thought I should be happy for all the nice times we had, and think about them instead, but that way has never worked for me.

At least I didn't waste the time we had together protecting myself against the separation to come. Except for the incident of seeing that you're as human as I am, Dad, it was an exceptionally happy three weeks.

Who said it was a sin to cry, anyway?

Love,
Ruth Ellen

MARCH, 1971

Dear Mom and Dad,

In a few days we go back to the States. It will be hard to leave, but it will be good to complete Dave's training.

I can't tell you how wonderful it has been to be home. I'm so glad that my husband finally knows where I come from!

Love,
Ruth Ellen

11

THE DOCTOR'S WIFE

JUNE, 1971

Dear Mom and Dad,

We made our big move to St. Louis a few days ago. Dave is excited about starting the last leg of his medical training, and I'm looking forward to staying home and being a true housewife and mother at last. We had a smooth trip down, if moving is ever smooth, but you know I'm not very efficient at settling in.

It's odd to be in a city where we don't know a single person. We didn't even know where to begin looking for a church. This morning we tried one that wasn't too friendly, so in the evening we drove around till we spotted a church with open doors. It's not far from our apartment and, since they invited us back, I think we'll probably go there.

Did I tell you that a kid Dave took care of in Liberia is coming to stay with us while he gets some treatment at the Shriners' Hospital? Momo has sickle cell anemia and needs treatment for a leg that has been deformed and shortened by a bone infection. We expect to pick him up at the airport next week. I hope to be settled by then!

Love,
Ruth

JULY, 1971

Dear Mom and Dad,
People warned me that Dave's internship would be a hard time for me, but I didn't believe them. Medical school wasn't as bad as we'd been told, and I figure after all I've been through, I'm tough enough to cope with anything.

But it's back to that old game of trying to measure up on the outside when inside I'm something else. I get the message that doctors' wives should be understanding, noble, selfless, brilliant, and truly happy for their husbands to be needed by so many. But, as usual, my brain and my feelings aren't synchronized. Instead of being understanding, I'm resentful of other people's claims on Dave's times. My conversation isn't brilliant; all I can think of to talk about is how many teeth Sheri has or whether it's better to take a walk in the direction of the fire station or the bagel shop.

Love,
Ruth

SEPTEMBER, 1971

Dear Mom and Dad,
I can't cope with Dave's schedule or with my isolation and loneliness. Having only a baby to talk to all day and taking

walks with my neighbor and her little boy to see the fire trucks are getting to me. I read the want ads and personal columns while sitting in my housecoat until ten or eleven o'clock each morning. I spend hours pushing Sheri in a cart around K-Mart, with two dollars in my pocket. I've even gotten addicted to the soap operas.

By the time Dave gets home, I'm so blue I'm sure he'd rather have stayed on call. It doesn't matter that all day I've been planning to be a wonderful wife that night—when he comes home two hours later than expected, or calls to be picked up and then keeps us waiting half an hour in front of the hospital, all my plans evaporate into frustration, anger, and depression. We have a quiet, rotten evening.

When he leaves the next morning, I'm sorry and vow never to repeat the cycle. I know it's not Dave's fault that another patient came in after he called me, or whatever. I even make a great meal and clean the house, some days, but the depression can start all over each evening for the slightest reason.

I feel totally out of control. Do you think I'm going crazy?

Love,
Ruth

OCTOBER, 1971

Dear Mom and Dad,

I've prayed myself sick asking God to change my behavior, but it still gets worse. I'm sure if I were as spiritual as I thought, I wouldn't be this depressed. How many hundreds of testimonies have I heard about the joy that Jesus gives? He surely isn't giving it to me right now—or maybe I just don't know how to receive it.

If I try to tell Dave what I'm thinking, he feels bad, because it seems like it's all his fault for being gone so much. When I reach the point where I have to tell him or explode, I do end up blaming him. Who or what else can I blame in this whole sorry mess? And who else can I talk to?

I can't tell Dave's mom, because I don't want her to know I'm so rotten to her poor son. And you're in Africa; what can you do? And besides, the less I like myself, the more I find myself blaming you for the way I am. I keep thinking that if you hadn't left me, or if you had done something differently, then I wouldn't be the way I am.

Actually, I'm pretty furious about the whole family thing. I have such a big family, and yet there's not a single one of you I dare tell how lousy this year is for me. So what if we all say we love each other? What good is that doing me now? We never seem to be together when we need each other most.

Love,
Ruth

NOVEMBER, 1971

Dear Mom and Dad,

This month Dave is on call every other night. I hardly see him two or three functioning hours out of forty-eight. I've asked other residents' wives how they cope with this awful schedule, and they all have wonderful answers. They set time aside to do special things with their husbands. They do crafts, refinish furniture, redecorate their houses. Always something creative, self-fulfilling, and terrific. It depresses me completely.

When we decide to do something special, an emergency keeps Dave from being there. When I go to a macrame class and buy the string for a plant hanger, I end up with a hopeless mess of tangled knots. When I tried to recover our grubby couch, it ended up looking anything but professional. The corners don't quite hit the edges right and the cushion covers are too loose. Instead of turning my living room into a master-piece from *House Beautiful*, we now look more like rummage sale castoffs than before.

While the other wives are taking all those enriching courses, I can't get past Sesame Street and Captain Kangaroo. Many of the other wives have children, too, so I've asked them how they have time for all these other wonderful activities. Then they tell me how marvelously their kids are doing in nursery school or day care centers. I'm beginning to think I'm depriving Sheri of her birthright by keeping her home with me, instead of sending her to a program where she can be reading novels by age two.

When I question my capabilities as a mother, some others tell me I'm not doing very well at being a wife, either. They say I'd be happier if I insisted that David put away his own laundry and shared in the cooking and cleaning. After all, he's getting clothes dirty, eating food, and helping to mess the place up. They think I'm unhappy because I've allowed myself to become a doormat. And here I thought that doing these things for David when he's so busy was the one way I could be a good wife.

This is the most confusing time of my life so far—how strange that it should come right after I thought I had gotten so many things together in Africa. The familiar voices inside me are screaming that if I'd just try a little harder by doing this or that, I wouldn't feel this way. But changing outside things has never changed inside things for me yet. It's the old boarding school feeling—everyone else is making it; why can't I?

Love,
Ruth

NOVEMBER, 1971

Dear Mom and Dad,

I'm beginning to understand why people commit suicide. It's because there's no hope left.

My trying hasn't changed a thing. My prayers bounce back off the walls and mock me. I've read every how-to book available on depression, marriage, and motherhood, but they just pile on more guilt.

I've thought of leaving Dave—not because I actually want to leave him, but to make a statement that somebody will hear.

"I'm lost. I have no idea where to turn. Can't anybody help me?" But when I think of leaving, I can't figure out where to go. You're in Africa. I doubt that Mom Van Reken would be thrilled to take me in, if I've just left her son! I have too much pride to go to any of my friends. And besides, I know perfectly well that as soon as I begin to pack my bags, I'll start crying and have to unpack.

It seems so unfair to drag David's life down with the weight of mine. I've actually wondered what it would be like to take pills and never wake up. But in my heart I know that wouldn't solve anything. I have a child I'm responsible for, and I want to see her grow up. And I want to live, if I can be the person that I've always thought I had the potential to be. But right now that seems likes a hopeless dream.

The thread I'm hanging on to is an intellectual belief that God still has a purpose for my life. I can't imagine how He can ever put all the pieces back together and make me whole, but it's my only hope. I told Him today that He could forget helping *me* to do better—there's nothing left of me to help. If He doesn't do something new, I'm finished.

Love,
Ruth

DECEMBER, 1971

Dear Mom and Dad,

A tiny ray of light broke through today; I'm not sure what it will amount to. In Sunday school, the teacher asked for prayer requests. Linda, a woman I've often seen there, asked for prayer because her mom was coming to visit. She said there are some tensions in their relationship, and she wanted God to heal the situation. She got a little teary as she talked, and you could tell she spoke from deep in her heart.

I've never heard so personal a request before in *any* group, missionaries included. Usually there are requests for the sick, work, and the lost, but those praying never seem to have any needs. And if they aren't needy, how can I let on that I am? I've always played the game like all the rest. But after Linda finished, I took a little courage from her example and thought, *I'll tell them a little, but I'll say it so they won't know how bad I really feel.*

"Maybe you could pray for me, too. My husband has a lot of time on call, and I'm struggling with that a bit." But would you believe I started to cry with just those few simple words? I was so embarrassed and sorry I'd given in to the urge to say anything. Now they all know how weak I am.

Afterward Linda came up and invited me to her house for coffee this week. I'm scared, because I know she figures I have a problem and wants to help. I'm not sure I'm ready to share. After all, we Frames (I still am one, even if I did change my name) are strong. Others come to us for advice.

But I know I need a friend, so I'll have to take the risk. I hope I can get by without her seeing too deeply inside.

Love,
Ruth

Dear Mom and Dad,

I went to Linda's today and, sure enough, she wondered if I were having a problem. I went on a bit about Dave's schedule and how I did feel a bit lonely. I said I knew I shouldn't mind, because he was helping people, and she stopped me right there.

"Why shouldn't you mind?" she said. "Would you understand if someone else felt that way?"

Well, of course I would, but this was different.

"What makes you think you're supposed to be more perfect than anyone else?" she asked.

I said I didn't think I was supposed to be perfect, but I should be able to tolerate his schedule better.

Linda wouldn't let me off the hook. Every time I mentioned a feeling I shouldn't have, she stopped me. She didn't think it was any big deal that I have all these horrible, awful feelings.

In fact, she thinks I'm acting out of pride, to think I should be above them all!

This is certainly new to me. She didn't even seem to think my Christianity was in question because of my struggles. Sometimes I got mad when she wouldn't let me spiritualize why I shouldn't feel a certain way.

I'm not sure I want to go back. I can't say I got a lot of sympathy, but I got acceptance. And challenge. Linda has offered to baby-sit Sheri every afternoon while I visit Momo in the hospital, so I probably can't avoid her.

Love,
Ruth

Dear Mom and Dad,

Linda said her home was available anytime. At first I thought she was just saying that, but she seems to mean it. She continues to offer me friendship, even when I decline her invitations because I don't want to intrude into her family time (or is it because I'm afraid of her perceptiveness?). Even her husband and sons treat us like extended family; they've asked me over for Christmas Eve, since Dave will be on call.

I'm still not sure if it's right, or safe, to express feelings that I've kept buried for so long, but Linda won't let me retreat. When I try to couch things in my usual fashion, she takes my feelings and puts them into words that identify what's behind them.

"Sounds like you were pretty angry about [whatever it was]," she'll say. Now, how did she know that? I only said I was a little upset. It's frightening, but I have to admit that it feels like releasing the valve on a pressure cooker. Finally the steam has somewhere to go, before the lid gets blown all the way off.

Love,
Ruth

Dear Mom and Dad,

My Sunday school teacher called the other day to see how I was doing. How humbling to be seen by others as a person obviously needing help! I guess I should be thankful, as I had too much pride to ask for it.

As we talked, I confided to him that I felt worse for David, because I don't think I can ever be a proper doctor's wife. The doctor's world is one of china and silver, and I'm still the girl from a world of cement floors. I keep thinking that Dave should have married someone who could cope better with all this.

My teacher asked me if I believed God had led David and me together.

"We thought so at the time," I answered, "but now I'm not so sure."

"Ruth," he said, "if God put you and Dave together, then you're exactly what he needs, and he's exactly what you need."

When I think of how difficult I've been to live with this year, I can scarcely believe that—but it's another ray of hope. I put a sign on my mirror: "You're exactly what he needs." I wonder if Dave has any idea why it's there! Even though I'm learning to express myself to these friends, I'm no more honest about my feelings with Dave than I ever was with you. Why is it so hard to talk to the people I love?

Love,
Ruth

FEBRUARY, 1972

Dear Mom and Dad,

Although bits of healing are taking place, I still struggle with boredom and lack of purpose. I asked God to lift these for me (as I have before), and the answer that came to me was to look for a part-time job.

That didn't seem very spiritual! After all, Sheri's not even one-and-a-half, and I thought good wives and mothers didn't work. But I couldn't shake the thought, so I finally went over to Barnes Hospital, and they hired me for just two evenings a week and no weekend calls. It was unbelievably simple.

It hurts my perception of myself as a wonderful mother to acknowledge that I need to get out—but God knows me better than I want to admit!

Love,
Ruth

Work was very helpful. I liked going out and function-ing with my own identity again. It also helped me struc-ture my time at home better. But it seemed that for every feeling I got out in the open, there were three more lurking behind. All the things that went down into that pot years before wanted to come out at once. I tried to keep the lid on and only let one or two escape at a time. If they all came out at once, I feared I'd be burned and scarred forever.

MAY, 1972

Dear Mom and Dad,

Last month we went to Dave's brother's wedding, and I was a bear again. Sheri hadn't napped, and she screamed during the whole plane ride. I resented Dave's need to sleep, even though he'd been up all night on call. I resented his folks' attempts to be helpful with my over-tired child when we arrived. I resented everything about anything.

Now I know that I was newly pregnant at the time, but I'm still ashamed of my behavior. Even when I think about you, I feel an undercurrent of anger. I can't pin it on anything specific, though I look for things to blame it on. I don't like feeling this way, but I don't know what to do about it.

Love,
Ruth

JANUARY, 1973

Dear Mom and Dad,

Rachel was born yesterday. Another wonderful experience of new life and hope. She's a real cutie, naturally, and Dave was with me again in the delivery room.

When I held her today, I realized that she's my second daughter, just as I am yours. It's hard to believe that I was as tender and precious to you as she is to me, but I know I must have been. It makes me sad to think of the many, many years of separation that lie between us.

Love,
Ruth

JUNE, 1974

Dear Mom and Dad,

The last two years of Dave's residency have been much better than the first. His call schedule was less demanding, and I've been more emotionally even. My main concern now is that I'm not sure we can still be missionaries, as we've always planned. If I'm as "untogether" as I now perceive myself, how can I presume to be anything for anyone else?

Dave has hardly been to church these last three years because he's either on call, just getting off call, or going in for rounds. We haven't exactly lost the faith, but the light is dim. Perhaps we are only meant to send others. I can't imagine that there's much left in us to offer.

By the way, we'll be moving to Portsmouth, Virginia, for Dave's stint in the Navy. I had to look it up on a map!

Love,
Ruth

P.S. I'm trying to match you in spacing my children two years apart. We'll be having our third when we get to Virginia. Glad you'll be home next year.

12

LESSONS FROM PORTSMOUTH

JULY, 1974

Dear Mom and Dad,

Thanks for planning the week for all of our family to be together. It's always special to spend time with each other, but sometimes I feel there are underlying tensions to our reunions. A lot of leftover feelings are still lying there unspoken from our growing up together and yet apart.

Some are probably hard feelings. For example, I don't believe I was very sensitive to Chuck and Tom when they arrived fresh from Africa on their own. I loved them and was glad to see them, and I'm sure I gave them lots of advice, but I doubt I was tuned in to what it was really like for them. My own world consumed my attention. To have me as one of their surrogate moms must have been a trial.

When Alice and Marj arrived, I identified with them more strongly—perhaps because they are girls, perhaps because I was older. But, in not wanting them to repeat all my mistakes, I wonder if I came across as too knowing and made them feel totally inferior to this older sister.

Whatever the causes, I had a feeling all week long of having fun, sharing our meals and recreation times, but keeping a carefully protected distance with each other on certain issues. I still have an underlying anger; when it comes out in sarcastic or derogatory comments, it hurts my younger brothers and sisters. I sound disloyal and unloving, but I'm really not. I love each one of you so much, yet I find that small things trigger strong feelings. The restlessness inside remains at a low boil. Sure wish I could find the switch to turn it off.

Love,
Ruth

Dear Mom and Dad,

We landed in Portsmouth safe and sound after some car trouble in West Virginia. Have we got the neatest house! It's a renovated Early American style, fully carpeted and draped. I've bought my first new furniture: a couch, chair, and dinette set.

Dave and I have always felt we shouldn't put our money into expensive things, since we plan to be missionaries—but to be very honest, it has bothered me a lot. Everything we have is so old looking and mix-and-match, with a lot less match than mix! The other doctors and their wives always seem to have nicer furniture, apartments, and all the rest. It's that old "why do we have to be different?" feeling.

Anyhow, that's changed now. With Dave's increase in salary, it seemed we could surely afford a couple of new things. It doesn't seem to be a sin for other Christians to have them, so why should it be for us?

By the way, I am thinking we probably had our "call" wrong. There are an awful lot of needs here in the States. We're probably more suited for staying here than for going overseas to missions. Besides, Dave has the potential to make a lot of money, and we could support several missionaries instead of just being there ourselves. Don't you agree?

Love,
Ruth

OCTOBER, 1974

Dear Mom and Dad,

This house is wonderful! I even felt "equal enough" to invite the pediatric department here for the monthly social. To my great surprise, the lure of *things* is suddenly very strong. My brain knows they aren't supposed to be important, but now that they are suddenly within my grasp, I realize how I've secretly coveted them for years. After doing without while others have so much, it feels as if it should finally be my turn.

Our new furniture is so pretty. I want more. The Exchange sells name brand clothes I've never worn before, and at reasonable prices. Mom, I hate to tell you this, but I think there is at least some difference between these clothes and bargain basement specials!

The only problem is that this house is consuming vast quantities of energy, due to poor insulation. Our electricity bill is about eight to ten times what it was for our small place in St. Louis. Dave thinks maybe we should move to a cheaper place. He says if God still wants us to go into missions, we need to get out of debt from medical school during this time, as we'd originally planned. Our utility bills are eating up all the extra.

I think we were probably all wrong about the idea of missions in the first place. I'm certainly no great spiritual example. I still struggle with depression, though it's not as hopeless as the first year in St. Louis. I hate the thought of having to raise support, when for the first time in my life there is the prospect of having more money than just what I need to squeeze out the essentials of life.

Even though Dave thinks we should move, I can't bear the thought. We've just settled in, the baby is due next week, and I hate moving, anyway. But when he has such spiritual reasons, I can't tell him I don't want to move. So I'm fudging . . . I told him we should pray about it.

Love,
Ruth

NOVEMBER, 1974

Dear Mom and Dad,

You won't believe what happened today—we got an eviction notice! Our landlord has gone bankrupt and is selling his other houses, and he needs this one for himself. We have six weeks to move.

I'm livid! After I've just painted everything, pulled all the weeds, and worked to get everything organized! He must have known this when he rented the house to us—at the time he said not to worry about a lease, because in this part of the country things were done by "gentlemen's agreements." We were fools to believe him.

I felt like taking a black paint brush and making huge X's on all the walls, or shredding the curtains with some kind of hooks. Dave wasn't home when the letter came, so I stewed around until he arrived. When he walked through the door, I shoved the letter in his face. "Look at this!"

After he read it, he said, "Well, I guess that's our answer."

I couldn't believe what I was hearing. "Can't you *do* something?" I cried. "He had no right to do this. He said we could be here for two years. It's not fair!"

Dave looked at me. "Ruth, I don't know what you're so upset about. We prayed, didn't we? God answered."

How dared he be so calm—or so *right*? Why were my feelings always at such odds with the rational way of looking at things?

It was then I realized I'd never prayed really looking for (or wanting) an answer. I knew what *I* wanted; I only prayed to appease David. I forgot God might actually be listening on the other side.

I'll be more careful how I pray in the future.

Love,
Ruth

Dear Mom and Dad,

Stephanie Lynn entered the world on November 29. She's beautiful. It surprises me how each of my daughters is such an individual, and each so wonderful! Actually, I was expecting a boy—with you and Mae Beth both having two girls and then a boy, I just presumed I would, too. Guess I broke tradition, but we love her dearly.

We stopped on the way home from the hospital to look at a town house Dave had seen advertised. I was pretty tired when I got home. It was great to have Mom Van Reken and Aunt Jean here this week. They've been a wonderful help, but tomorrow they leave, and we're on our own.

Love,
Ruth

DECEMBER, 1974

Dear Mom and Dad,

I got a call from Mae Beth last night. When she found out Mom Van Reken couldn't stay any longer, she decided to come and help me. I can't believe it! Imagine still needing your older sister when you're twenty-nine!

I feel guilty accepting her help when she's got three small kids of her own, but she says she wants to come. They'll get here later today.

Her offer made me feel warm all over. Here's a time when I need my family, and they'll actually be here!

> Love,
> Ruth

Dear Mom and Dad,

It's a good thing Mae Beth came, as I got a fever and have been totally incapacitated for several days. All I've done is stay in bed and read stories to Rachel (who does look forlorn and bewildered by all this), nurse Stephanie, watch Sheri play with her cousins, and try to sleep. Mae Beth has done everything else.

I feel bad to see her work so hard, but I don't know how I would have managed without her. And it's been a very special feeling to be sisters again in a true, and even new, sense.

Thanks for all the sisters and brothers you gave me.

> Love,
> Ruth

JANUARY, 1975

Dear Mom and Dad,

In spite of the fact that Dave wanted our move to reduce expenses, I kept trying to find a house comparable to the one we were in. After all, I definitely need more space, now that I have three kids. We kept looking in the suburb where the other doctors live. One night we came home and decided to take a place we had just looked at. It would only increase our expenses, but I didn't care. It was what I needed.

As we began to talk about the new place, one thing became clear. We weren't dealing with true need, but with a whole lot of *want*. What we *need* is a roof over our heads, a warm place for the girls to stay, and some place I can do the wash and take care of the family. We don't even need to worry about school districts, since we'll leave Portsmouth before Sheri starts first grade.

I had to admit we've lived happily and comfortably in far more modest situations than at present, with all of our needs met. It was only pride that was driving me to want the same kind of house as everyone else.

And meanwhile, the strong missions emphasis at Tabernacle Church is making me face again the possibility that God may, in spite of all my deficiencies and excuses, be calling us to go overseas. If so, we must get out of debt.

The end result was that we found a small house in a community where most are enlisted men in the Navy or longtime residents. The rent and utilities together are the same as the rent in our other house.

I still fight embarrassment when people come to visit and see me living differently from what they expected. But each time I'm forced back to a basic issue: Am I only worth something with the right house to back me up, or is my worth in Jesus and who He made me to be? Not a bad thing for me to wrestle with.

Love,
Ruth

JUNE, 1975

Dear Mom and Dad,

Our stay in Portsmouth has become the most incredibly rich spiritual time we've had since getting married. Tabernacle Church feeds us spiritually as we've never been fed before, not only in its teaching, but in its whole approach to life. We see a whole community of believers living by faith together. They have an extremely strong emphasis on missions, and the old challenge is returning.

Dave is on call only a time or two a month now, so he comes home at a regular hour and plays with the girls. We have supper on schedule, and then he builds a fire in the fireplace with the girls as I wash the dishes. We're finally a normal family!

God is even using the location of our home as an opportunity for ministry. Since our home isn't a fancy one, people of all different occupations and walks of life aren't afraid to visit. We have lots of drop-in company.

Jesus seems alive and exciting again—even some of our friends from the hospital have come to Christ. We are back to actively considering missions, so we are paying off the debts. It's amazing what yielding to the Lord can do, even when I didn't particularly want to!

Love,
Ruth

FEBRUARY, 1976

Dear Mom and Dad,

Our nearly two years here have gone so fast; it's been a terrific time in our lives. We've been accepted to go to candidate school at the mission the month after we finish with the Navy. Wish we could go earlier, but we have to wait until Dave is finished with his commitment here.

Since we have no other plans between candidate school and leaving for Africa, the church feels we should proceed in faith and plan to be on the charter flight in September. That leaves only six weeks from the end of the school until leaving, but we feel God would have us trust Him. The church has asked us to join in their missions emphasis week this year as missionary candidates, even though it's not official yet. That's faith on their part! We're excited about the opportunity.

And the neat thing about leaving in September is that, if you come home for the summer as you plan, we'll be going back together. It's about time!

Love,
Ruth

MARCH, 1976

Dear Mom and Dad,

This is Missions Week at church. The first Sunday Dave had one of his rare call days. I spoke to a Sunday school class about how great it is to serve Jesus, had enlightening talks with many, and felt totally spiritual and useful for Jesus. Going home, we stopped at McDonald's to buy lunch, so we could take it to Dave at the hospital and see him. The girls all fell asleep en route, and by the time I got there, it was a bit of work to wake them all, take them in, and not drop the lunch!

I asked a corpsmen to call Dave, and he said fine. We went to Dave's office to wait—and wait—and wait. By now the girls were fussy, the food was cold, and I was getting perturbed. I went to look for Dave, and when I saw the same corpsman, he said, "Oh, I'm so sorry. I forgot to tell your husband." Great.

Dave appeared a few minutes later. He took one bite of his Big Mac, and someone rushed up. "Dr. Van Reken, we need you in the emergency room."

He looked at me apologetically. "Honey, I think I'm going to be tied up a while. Why don't you take the girls home and I'll call you later?"

I was furious. I knew he couldn't help it, but feelings from his internship days, long forgotten, flooded over me. I knew in that instant that if we were missionaries I would live as an eternal "intern's wife," and I didn't want to do it. God has taken my family all my life. He can't have David.

I didn't speak to David, or God, for two days. Meanwhile, I was supposed to be the budding missionary at church. It was terrible. By Tuesday I knew I had to do something about this conflict. I didn't want to tell the pastor, because then he'd know how unspiritual I was, and I was sure the church would instantly drop our support.

I chose a moment to get next to the special speaker during a luncheon. At first I talked in great generalities about "How do you and your wife cope with the separations, since you're gone on so many speaking tours?"

He gave the same old wonderful answer about setting times to get away together after they're reunited, etc. It wasn't very helpful. Finally I told him exactly what was bothering me.

He looked me straight in the eye and said, "Ruth, the problem is that you've never given David totally to Jesus. If you had, you would view any time you have with him as God's gift to you. You're telling God that you need a certain percentage of Dave's time. If you get only nine percent, instead of the ten percent you think you deserve, you're so unhappy about what you lost that you can't enjoy what you have."

I knew in that instant that he was absolutely right. I've had to give you, my sisters, and my brothers all to Jesus before. But in my heart, I've felt God owes me at least my husband's time. After all these years of trying various methods to cope with Dave's schedule, I now feel a deep relief. This time the disease was hit, not the symptoms only.

When I tried to explain to Dave, he said he didn't want me to give him away. It's not that I don't need him. But the question is, can I trust God to meet my needs for companionship, or do I have to strive for myself?

Jesus says we will lose what we try to keep, and only keep what we give to Him. I've thought of it in all sorts of ways before, but I never saw how David has been the one thing I've wanted to keep just for myself all these years. So today David had to join the list of family given to God. It's that same old area that God always seems to go after—I didn't realize it wasn't over yet.

Love,
Ruth

MARCH, 1976

Dear Mom and Dad,

Have you ever been stripped naked in front of seven hundred people? I mean naked to your soul?

It happened to me on the last day of the mission conference. After my talk with the speaker on Tuesday, I felt so free and

happy. Having surrendered everything I know about to Christ,
I experienced deep peace. I didn't have to guard and protect
for myself any longer. I enjoyed every minute with Dave, and
the meetings lifted and challenged me. I felt ready to give my
life totally away to Jesus.

On the way to the service the last morning, I asked Dave if
we could give money to the speaker, since he'd been so helpful
to me. Dave agreed, and I put a check in my purse for the man.

The sermon title was "The Alabaster Box." The speaker told
of the woman who gave Jesus her most precious ointment.
Everyone around said, "What a waste," but Jesus said nothing
precious is ever wasted on Him. The whole world would know
of what she had done. The speaker made the application that
in every one of our lives, God requires a precious thing. For
each of us it's different, but it's always precious; it's the one
thing we think we can't bear to be without. It can be profession,
money, family, or whatever. When we give it to Him, the
world around will surely say we are fools, but Jesus says, "No,
I will take that very thing to make it bring great honor to My
Name."

As the man spoke, I knew good and well where he'd gotten
the idea for his sermon! I felt almost smug, thinking of how
useful my story must have been for him in his preparation. But
in a million years I couldn't have been prepared for what happened next.

He continued, "Just this week I was talking to" [*surely he
won't let them know who*] "the wife of one of the missionary
candidates" [*maybe people will think it's one of the other two*]—
"who was struggling with . . ." and on he went until there was
no question whom he was describing. After all, there was only
one of us going to Africa with a doctor for a husband. No
names were mentioned, of course! He told of how losing family
had been such a hard thing for me all my life, and how I didn't
want to give my husband to Jesus. Everything I'd said to him
was replayed back to that huge congregation! There we were,
in the second row from the front. Dave sat like stone. Every
eye was boring into my head from behind. I wished the floor
would open and swallow me whole.

My first thought was, *Buddy, you ain't gettin' a dime from me today*. Then the tears started. If I cried when I got spanked in front of the class in first grade, you should have seen me today! The same feelings of overwhelming shame swept over me, and I just couldn't stop.

The story went on and on, at least it seemed that way to me. The speaker issued an invitation at the end, asking all who were willing to give their precious things to Jesus to stand up. All over the audience people stood. I knew God was work-ing, but that didn't take away the hurt.

And I thought to myself, *Well, now that they all know exactly how rotten and unspiritual I am, nobody in this church will give us any support*. It's definitely not the recommended way to do deputation! I couldn't imagine how I'd get out after the service. I finally got pious enough to say, "Well, God, if you can use this in someone else's life, then I'm willing to be exposed." But it still felt like a knife dividing my soul.

At the end, I tried to creep away. Some who passed pretended they hadn't figured out who in the world he had been speaking about. But one of my friends came up, gave me a huge hug, and asked, "Did you give him permission, Ruth?" I could only shake my head no and head for the nursery to get my babies.

As I went into the nursery, the Lord's voice spoke to me as clear as a bell: "Go give the man that money."

"Are You kidding, Lord? After what he just did to me?"

"Go, Ruth. Now!"

I sure didn't want to, but sometimes His voice is so clear there is no way to disobey except through total defiance. I went back into church and found the man talking to someone else. He stopped, came over to me, and said, "I hope you didn't mind, Ruth. It just seemed that was what God had for me to say."

I realized that he may not have even planned to use my story, but in the speaking it happened, but I couldn't say I didn't mind. I muttered something about hoping God would use it, gave him the check, and fled.

Going back, Dave introduced me to some people who had just offered to take on some of our support. I couldn't believe it! After all that? And several more offered the next day.

I'm still feeling bruised, but I learned some important things through this experience. For one thing, I needed to give the speaker that check not for his sake, but for mine. Giving him the check forced me to consciously forgive him. If I'd carried away the bitterness that I felt while he was talking, I would have completely corroded away inside by now.

For another thing, I realized that the whole church now knows my worst secret and they still love me! It's amazing. How could they want someone who's so totally untogether to represent them as a missionary? Many of the masks I've worn for so long were ripped off by force. The awful, naked ugliness of my soul was exposed, and I was still accepted! I can't believe it.

Love,
Ruth

APRIL, 1976

Dear Mom and Dad,

One of my friends has been after David and me for a year to go to something called "Marriage Encounter." It's some kind of seminar on better expression of feelings inside a marriage. I've always put her off with, "Yes, it's a good idea. We'll have to do it sometime." David always says he doesn't have many feelings, and I don't know how many more of mine I could face!

Today she called to say she's made arrangements for a baby-sitter so we can go a particular weekend. The only way to get out of it is to be extremely rude, so I guess we're going. I'm a little scared.

Love,
Ruth

Dear Mom and Dad,

The Marriage Encounter weekend was mind boggling. I'm emotionally and physically drained from its intensity, yet I'm excited about what I've learned.

Since the weekend was led by a Catholic priest, I entered it with some caution. Would he try to convert us? And how could he lead a seminar like this, anyway—he's not married. But as the participating couples presented their dialogues to us, two life-changing concepts came through to me.

The first was, "There is no morality to feelings." I met that with great doctrinal reservation at first. What about the verse, "If you lust after a woman in your heart, you've already committed adultery"? Or, "If you hate someone, you've already committed murder?" Wasn't this a watering down of the Word?

I listened carefully as they continued to explain. "There is no morality in the feeling itself, it is the choice of what you *do* with that feeling that becomes a moral issue." Hate can come in a flash; it's the nursing of it that turns it into mental or actual murder. Lustful thoughts will come, but the choice is to dwell on them and turn them into action, or admit them and let them go.

It made sense. If feelings by themselves were sinful (as I've always felt), wouldn't Christ's temptations have been sin? Yet we're told He was tempted in all points as we are. He must have felt despair, but He was not ruled by those feelings.

The second major thing they said was, "You own your feelings. Others don't cause them." They didn't say there weren't *reasons* for our feelings, but that we choose our reaction to each situation. I wasn't too sure about that at first, either. If they only knew my situation, surely they'd think I had some justification for all the anger I feel so often! But as I thought about it, I had to admit they were right. The same set of circumstances can cause totally different reactions in me, depending on what's going on inside. Even a child crying at night can make me feel warm and protective one time and frustrated to pieces the next.

They also said that a big problem we all have is feeling guilty for all the other feelings we have that we think we shouldn't have—especially feelings that "a good Christian would never feel." Do you realize that I've spent my life feeling guilty? I'm forever saying, "I know I shouldn't feel this way, but—" Dave says I don't feel good if I don't feel guilty!

The guilt takes so many forms:

Guilt for being sad at leaving home when I should have been braver, because it was what God wanted.

Guilt for wishing I had things as nice as other kids, when I already had more than the starving masses.

Guilt for the anger I felt at you for leaving me, when I knew you truly loved me and only did it because you believed it was God's will.

Guilt for feeling disappointment and rage when my special times with Dave were spoiled by patients' needs.

Guilt for wanting to kick and scream at Dave when he fell asleep in the bathtub, after I'd waited to talk to him for two whole days.

Of course I believed it was God's will for you to go. How dare I be angry about that? What are my needs for private conversation and supper with my husband, compared to some child whose very life is in danger? Of course I should be sympathetic and understanding when Dave hasn't slept for thirty-six hours. But the guilt always tried to shift the blame onto somebody else—to you, to Dave, to any situation around. Something to justify how I felt. But in the end it always comes back to me. Why can't my feelings match what my brain knows to be true?

But these people have given me some startling ideas. Is it really okay to admit I have felt hurt, or rejected, or pained in a situation as a matter of fact, rather than as a matter of shame or blame? I don't know. A whole new world has been opened to me, but I'm not sure how to walk in it yet.

Love,
Ruth

13

ALMOST A MISSIONARY

MAY, 1976

Dear Mom and Dad,

Healing doesn't come all at once, but each new lesson prepares the way for future revelations. If I hadn't first learned about admitting my feelings for what they are, I don't think I could have borne what God has shown me this time.

You always called me a "worrywart," even when I was a small child. Through the years that worrying has stayed with me. If I read about someone's baby getting killed, I know it will happen to mine one day. For years I've prayed about these depressions and anxieties. I've also prayed not to get mad so easily, but my anger continues to flash out in stupid situations.

Tonight I was preparing a talk for the Mothers' Club at church, on "Helping Your Child Develop a Good Self-Image." (I'm the expert, right?!) I was checking out some books, dutifully jotting down notes, and I came across this statement: "Circumstances don't create your spirit, they reveal it." This fits right in with what I've learned about owning my own feelings. Then I read how repressed anger can come out in depression and anxiety. I wrote that down, too—for my talk, of course!

Then out of the blue it hit me: I get angry because I *am* angry. God showed me this huge, awful, black hole of anger deep inside me. It's the pot where everything went for so many years. My depressions and anxieties are only the lid on that pot.

Perhaps since I was raised a Christian and never did "terrible, awful sins," I've never realized before that I am a sinner not only because of what I do, but because of what I am. For years, I've been trying to treat a cancer with band-aids. They cover the hole for a while, but they don't touch the disease at its source.

It wasn't easy to face who I really am, and I didn't know what to do about it. So I did the only thing possible; I told God I'd never known before that minute exactly what darkness was in my soul. Even when I first received Christ, I was not as aware of my state of being a sinner as I am tonight. I realized that committing sins isn't what makes me a sinner; it's my heart condition that does it. What I do only stems from that. (Come to think of it, that's what the Bible has said all along! How have I missed seeing it so clearly all this time?)

Instead of asking Him to help me not to get angry, not to get depressed, not to worry, I asked Him to treat the disease—to do the surgery necessary to remove it. A verse came to me then: "Perfect love casts out fear." It made sense. If repressed anger causes anxiety and fear, then replacing that anger with God's love will take care of the fear. But how does it work? Will it work? I surely hope so.

Love,
Ruth

JUNE, 1976

Dear Mom and Dad,

I'm realizing that my unacknowledged anger has been what's bred my spirit of resentment. And that resentful spirit will destroy me faster than any of the actual situations I've ever been through. As I think about where all this anger of mine came from, the most obvious source is all our separations—leaving me with mixed feelings about your return to the States again next week. Having finally recognized my feelings, what am I supposed to do about them?

I think the key may have something to do with forgiveness. I heard a woman say she'd had to learn to forgive many people in her life just for being who and what they were. To forgive a husband for being non-mechanical, for example, even though it makes life harder for the wife. To forgive a child for not being scholar material.

I have to go back and do a good bit of forgiving, especially in the areas where I felt pain even when it was never intended by those who caused it. The kids who laughed at my hairstyle; the teacher who wanted to pull my tooth; you, for sending me away because it seemed the best thing for me at that time; and all those who locked me up with pat answers or quick words of encouragement, when what I needed was understanding and a hug.

The verse comes to me, "Forgive us our trespasses, as we forgive those who trespass against us." I'm sure I've also hurt many others unintentionally, and sometimes intentionally, by my words and actions. I haven't always listened to the meaning behind the words of those with deep hurts. I need *your* forgiveness.

In spite of the turmoil I've felt these last few years, I do love you, and I know you love me, too. I've asked God to let me *feel* your love once again, instead of only knowing it. I can't imagine how He will do it, but I know I need it for my healing.

Love,
Ruth

God's answer to my prayer was prompt and specific. My mom and dad, tired from another term, walked into the mess of my trying to pack for our own trip to Africa. And the mess was worse because of my usual disorganized state. All the boxes yet to be labeled, shipping forms to be filled out, piles of stuff left yet to pack.

When I don't know how else to cope, I generally run away. This time I did it by leaving Mom and Dad to pack while I took the girls to a neighbor's birthday party. When I returned, Mom met me at the door and said they had decided to stay a little longer instead of leaving the next day.

I laughed. "Why? Don't think I can get my packing done by the end of the week?"

"Oh, uh, oh no," she replied. "We just thought we'd like to stay a little longer."

She never did lie well, and I love her for it. Of course they were staying to help me pack. But it wasn't just their wanting to help that touched me so deeply—it was when I asked her, "Mom, what about all the supporters you were going to visit over the next few days?"

She said, "We already called them and said we wouldn't be coming this time."

I think they were shocked when I burst into tears. I tried to explain about needing to know they loved me, but it was pretty garbled. Mom said, "But of course we love you."

Even at age thirty, my needs were more important to them than their ministry. I needed so badly to know that.

JULY, 1976

Dear Mom and Dad,

Now that God has started emptying this pot of stored-up feelings, He doesn't show any signs of quitting. I can't believe how much is in there.

Today at candidate school, we had a talk from another MK about sending our kids to boarding school. The speaker said that if parents are really positive, talk it up to the kids, write letters, etc., the child won't mind going and in fact will find it a lot of fun. His parents (who lived just twenty-five miles from the school) used to drive him out, unpack his things into the drawers, and slip away while he was playing. He'd hardly notice they had gone away.

As he talked, I felt something welling up inside of me. I wanted to scream "No, no, *no!* It's not that way for everyone." But I was stopped by that long-familiar feeling that I must be the only person alive who doesn't think boarding schools are 100% terrific.

When he finished, another member of our class said, "John, that was fine for you, because your parents could actually take you to the school. What about kids whose folks couldn't do that?"

John said, "Well, I did feel kind of sorry for the kids whose parents had to wave good-bye at the airplane."

Then the dam burst. I know I'm supposed to be a big girl now, but in that moment I was transported from that class in New Jersey back to the airport in Kano twenty-four years before. As always, you were brave and cheerful. As always, I was trying to be. I got into the little Cessna and put my belt on; they closed the doors and the plane started taxiing away. I turned for a last look. I guess you thought we were too far away to see, but in my last glimpse of you, Mom, I saw that Dad had his arm around your shoulder. You turned to him, put your head on his shoulder, and cried.

Maybe that was the first time I understood you were upset, too. I wanted them to stop the plane so I could run back and tell you I felt that way, too. At least we could have cried together. But the plane kept going. You were just a spot in the distance, and we never shared that moment.

Since by now the others in the class were wondering why I'd dissolved into such a water fountain in the middle row, I put my hand up. I had to let them know that not all kids are like John . . . and God gave me the courage to do just that.

I hope they don't think I was saying it's always wrong to send a kid to boarding school. I just want so much for parents to understand that because their child isn't crying outside doesn't mean he isn't feeling inside. Sometimes kids need comfort before encouragement.

Love,
Ruth

Sharing honestly with that group of missionary candidates wasn't easy, but they listened to what I had to say.

"John," I said, "I realize a great many kids seem to experience these wonderful, happy memories of boarding school. But I think the class should know that there are other kids like me. Maybe they'll have one someday.

"My parents did every single thing you said. They spoke of school positively, packed special things for me to open on the airplane, put letters in my suitcase. They never failed to write. They couldn't have done more to make it a positive experience. And I never questioned their love when they sent me off. It's only that it hurt. Every time I cried, somebody always tried to cheer me up. They gave me lots of encouragement. They said, 'Tomorrow will be better.' But I don't remember anyone ever sitting down and just crying with me, or even saying it was okay that I cried.

"Somehow the encouragement made it worse. It must be my fault I felt so bad, if everything about the whole situation was so good. What was the defect in my character? John, it just plain wasn't easy, at least for me."

There was an embarrassed but sympathetic silence. Then someone asked, "Are you saying you shouldn't have been sent to school?"

"I'm not saying that," I answered. "I'm confident that my parents sought God's will earnestly for us. The Bible says that God may require us to give up family

rights that we would normally choose to keep, for His sake and the Gospel's. It may well be God's plan for a child to go away to school. I'm just saying that the cheerleading approach to coping with it wasn't helpful for me. It locked me up even tighter."

"So what are parents supposed to do with someone like you?" they asked. "What would you have liked to have been different?"

"I needed to know I wasn't bad, or awful, or a silly baby for what I felt. I think if my parents, or housemother, or another adult missionary had been able to sit me in their lap, hold me tight and let me cry about it until I was finished, in the end I probably could have worked out the reasons for going by myself—or I would have been more ready to hear their reasons. At least I would have felt understood and not so terribly alone."

"Don't you think if you give a kid that much sympathy, it will make it harder for him to go?" someone wondered.

"I don't believe so. It will undoubtedly make it harder for the parents to send him, but it should be worth that extra cost to relieve the pressure of guilt their child is experiencing for feeling so bad about leaving. My greatest burden was trying to be on the outside what I thought I was supposed to be, even though I didn't feel that way inside. I didn't want to let my parents, or Jesus, down. That's a pretty heavy load for a little kid to carry."

It was hard being that vulnerable with a group of strangers, but the possibility of helping even one child be better understood and comforted made it worth the risk.

14

WHERE'S THE PERFECT MISSIONARY?

SEPTEMBER, 1976

Dear Mom and Dad,

I'm actually back in Africa as a full-fledged missionary. It was odd to be the one leaving this time. For the first time in all these years, my whole family will be in the States, while I'll be on the opposite side of the ocean.

Only one of our bags has arrived so far. I was so determined not to look like a missionary, even if I am one, but it didn't work out that way. I had packed only one skirt and blouse in the suitcase that came, so that's all I had to wear to a reception our first evening here. All the other women were wearing lovely African gowns or European clothes. How strange to have that old feeling of being dressed all wrong, when I was sitting in a whole pack of missionaries! God has some sense of humor.

Love,
Ruth

Dear Mom and Dad,

I think God was chiding me about my unacknowledged plan to show missionaries they don't have to dress ugly to be spiritual. (And either I remember wrong, or they have vastly improved since my day!)

First, our suitcases all arrived the day after I had nothing wonderful to wear to the reception. God kept them back only long enough for me to have that experience.

Second, I was chatting on the back porch yesterday when I smelled a caramel type odor. I checked the stove and all around but couldn't find anything burning. When it got worse, I went through the house. To my horror, I found that a brand new, white dress (that I haven't even worn here once) had slipped off its hanger and fallen onto the light bulb at the bottom of the closet. (We have to keep a light on to prevent mildew, since we live right on the beach.) It had a terrible scorch mark, exactly in the middle and right through the entire dress.

I felt sick. Mom Van Reken had bought the dress for my birthday, and it was truly beautiful. I'd even bought red shoes and accessories especially to go with it, and now it was fit only for rags. As I came out of the bedroom with the dress in hand, the radio began to play a Scripture chorus I'd never heard before: "In everything give thanks, for this is the will of God in Christ Jesus concerning you."

I wanted to smash the radio. What could a burned dress possibly have to do with God's will for me? He would never expect me to give thanks for that. Unfortunately, the chorus was so repetitive I was forced to consider again. Could it really be God's will that my sharpest outfit had just burned? If so, what was He trying to say?

I remembered the first night when I had nothing fantastic to make my debut with—now this. It seemed to me I heard Jesus saying: "Ruth, you still haven't truly settled who you are. In Portsmouth I had to show you that you weren't your house. Now I have to show you that you're not your clothes. I know you felt awful and ugly when you didn't have the same clothes the other kids did, but that never changed who you were. And even now, if you wear the most fantastic clothes any missionary has ever worn, it won't change anything about you. I've accepted you. There's nothing left to prove. You don't have to fight that part of your past anymore."

I know He's right . . . but I still plan to take the white dress apart and use it as a pattern to make another!

Love,
Ruth

OCTOBER, 1976

Dear Mom and Dad,

Some of the excitement of being here has worn off, and I'm having a few more struggles than I'd anticipated. For one thing, when it comes to living in Africa, I feel like a senior, or at least a junior. But since I'm a "new missionary," others see me as a freshman. It hurts my pride!

A lot of old resentments from my childhood are being stirred up again, as situations trigger a flood of memories long buried. There are things I always thought weren't fair, especially in the missionaries' relationships to the nationals. Giving missionary kids cold water if they want a drink, but telling nationals to go to the outside faucet. Calling national workers by their first names, while we expect them to call us Mr. and Mrs. or Miss.

Maybe I feel so strongly because you were a missionary kid yourself, Dad. I think the fact that you grew up with friends not of your own culture or race made you realize how, underneath all these superficial differences, people are all the same. I'm also frustrated because I know from the friends I grew up

with how very important these things are later. These same
nationals grow up either hating missionaries or loving them,
depending on how they are treated. And more importantly, it
affects how they see Jesus.

I feel I'm viewed as a troublemaker when I make suggestions
about small things that I think would improve our national/mis-
sionary relationships. And here I thought that when I returned
to Africa, I would at last think like everyone else.

Love,
Ruth

NOVEMBER, 1976

Dear Mom and Dad,

Another thing that keeps bothering me is my standard of
living. I thought all that had been dealt with in Portsmouth
when I changed houses. I laughed and told my friends, "It's a
good thing I'll be a poor missionary, so I won't have to struggle
about an appropriate Christian life-style. I won't have any
choice!"

It's one thing to choose to live with less and be rather noble
about it. But now I find that, having made those choices, I'm
still rich.

I have a bed for each of my kids and curtains on my windows,
while many nationals don't even have a cloth to cover the
floor where their children sleep.

The man painting our house doesn't have two dollars to
register his child for school—I have one hundred bars of soap
I brought for the next two years.

I cut a large piece of fat off some pork I bought, and threw
it away. The next day the man who helps me every morning
came to work. When he saw it, he was crushed. He couldn't
believe I would throw out what would have flavored many
helpings of soup for his rice.

Yesterday another missionary said I must be glad all my ship-
ment had arrived from home. I said that actually it was causing

me a lot of confusion, because of the great disparity between what I have and what all those around me don't have. He laughed and said, "Oh, you'll get used to that feeling soon enough."

The problem is, I'm not sure I should.

Love,
Ruth

DECEMBER, 1976

Dear Mom,

I'm not getting my act together very quickly. For one thing, I still don't have a job description. During the last six years they've pretty well nationalized the nursing. The only things I've tried to do haven't worked out with the children's schedule. And moms aren't particularly expected to work outside the home anymore; it's acceptable for them to stay home and care for their children. So I know the pressure I'm feeling to go to work is from within.

I lived for so many years with, "I don't know how your Mom does everything she does, and does it so well," that I came out assuming I could do the same. Maybe I wanted to prove that I could.

How could you always teach classes in Dad's school from the first day on? Then later you taught the four of us in the back of your regular classroom. You entertained regularly, marked papers faithfully, always had your private devotions in the morning and with Dad in the evening, took us on picnics, helped with the ladies' program at church, gave us music lessons, and were Dad's secretary. It all looked so effortless.

As it turns out, I'm not you. I seem to spend my life being interrupted and getting nothing accomplished. Four-year-old Rachel asked me recently when I was going to start being a missionary!

And I'm getting more and more critical all the time. Yesterday, I was saying to someone how criticism is generally a reflection of what a person doesn't like about himself. So I asked myself, what is it that I don't feel good about that is making me so critical of everyone else? Maybe, since I don't seem to be finding my own niche, I resent it when others have theirs. If I tear them down a bit, my own emptiness won't be so apparent.

I'm not sure what my cure will be, but it helps to have a diagnosis. I'm only sorry that, after God has shown me so much this past year, I can't rest in some semi-perfect state a little longer before I have to learn new lessons! Wish I were a better student.

Love,
Ruth

JANUARY, 1977

Dear Mom and Dad,
I had hoped that the airplane ride over would make me a perfect missionary inside and out, but apparently it didn't. It's odd that living in a Christian community can leave me feeling so unspiritual. Everyone here seems so super-spiritual that I don't dare tell them when I'm not coping well.

I miss our church fellowship from Portsmouth. At home I could call a friend, and she'd listen and encourage me. I never felt that my whole spirituality was being questioned. Here I get the feeling if I share any of my struggles, they'll turn up in the next prayer meeting ("The Alabaster Box" revisited?). Maybe that's not true, but there aren't many people with whom I am willing to risk sharing deeply yet.

At the New Year's Eve service last night, I asked God to make this a year in which we learn to show more love to each other here on the mission station. I felt Him pointing the finger back at me: was I willing for Him to start with me? Could it be more my problem than anyone else's?

I tried to tell Him I didn't need it nearly as much as many others I could list, but He was relentless. "If you're serious about wanting to see more love here, may I start by teaching you some things?"

How could I say anything but yes?

Love,
Ruth

FEBRUARY, 1977

Dear Mom and Dad,

Yesterday we were all packed to go away for a week's vacation. Dave had gone to the hospital to see someone when a resident and his wife came over to visit. I called to tell him, but there was no answer. When I called again ten minutes later, they said he was in the operating room with Ellsworth Balzer, who had just had an accident. I wasn't too concerned. Since Dave isn't a surgeon, I figured it must be for a few stitches or something. I waited a bit longer, growing more and more nervous. Suddenly the neighbors' son came flying up on his motorcycle. "Mr. Balzer's had a bad accident. They're looking for A+ blood. Rhoda's been hurt, too."

Not Uncle Ell! My heart started racing. *Please don't let it be too bad, God. What would Aunt Lois ever do without him?*

When I got to the hospital, I met Aunt Lois. Uncle Ell was in the operating room where five doctors were already at work on him. Rhoda was being X-rayed for a broken leg and arm.

People carried the word to church, where the evening service was about to begin. They asked for prayers and blood donors. Others went into the military mission in town to get donors from there as well.

I thought Aunt Lois would be beside herself, but she had an amazing spirit of peace. I've never seen anything like it. I prayed for that same peace but couldn't seem to find it.

In the middle of the night Uncle Ell quit breathing on his own, so he's on a respirator now. He received thirty-five units of blood through the night. Rhoda had her surgery about two a.m.

This morning Aunt Lois asked me to go into the operating room where Uncle Ell was still being kept. On the way, I got a phone call from Dave, who had gone home to check on the girls.

"Ruth, you had better come home for a few minutes. We were robbed last night."

How could God let two terrible things happen in the same night? I didn't mention it to Aunt Lois. When we were at Uncle Ell's side, she began praying out loud. "God, Ellsworth was Yours long before he ever was mine. It's not my desire for You to take him, but if that is Your will, then I give him back to you. But these are very expensive lessons. Don't let us waste them."

How could she be so accepting? I couldn't even accept that my belongings were gone, let alone a husband. When we left the operating room, I hurried home. What a terrible sight! The sheets were gone from off the beds, the closets emptied, radio space vacant, all the food and extra linens I'd prepared for the trip—everything was gone.

Uncle Ell was dying at the hospital; my house was in shambles. What could I do? Then that tune of a few weeks back came to me. "In everything give thanks, for this is the will of God in Christ Jesus concerning you." I couldn't say thanks *for* any of the situations, but I did realize that none of this could have happened without God allowing it.

Aunt Lois was right. These were expensive lessons. Whatever He wanted to say, I didn't want to have to hear it twice. So I said, "Jesus, I can't really thank you for the accident or the robbery, but I will thank you for what you want to show me in all of this. Only let me learn well, so I don't have to go through it again."

In a flash His answer came. "Ruth, your aunt just gave me her husband. You won't give me your sheets."

He was right. I was upset because, for the first time in my life, I had owned two sets of matching sheets for all my kids' beds, so I wouldn't have to wash and put them back the same day. Now all six sets were gone! But whose stuff was it, anyway?

Until that instant I hadn't realized how I compartmentalize things. The big things I've turned over to God—my husband, my kids, what I should do with my life. But I've held on to the little things. They seemed too insignificant to have any spiritual merit. In keeping them for myself, however, it's become harder to give when others have need.

I know I have lots more to learn from the experiences of the last twenty-four hours, but when I yielded to God's right to take away as well as to give me things, I had peace.

This afternoon some boys were fishing nearby and found quite a few of our things in a bush. We got back the essentials— some clothes (not my newest and best) and some of the sheets. I guess I didn't realize what the "essentials" were until today!

Love,
Ruth

Dear Mom and Dad,

Time feels suspended. How many years ago was Sunday? It's hard to know how to pray. If I just have enough faith, God says He will do anything. I've been trying very hard to believe for a miracle, but I remember how much I believed back in second grade, and Barbie still died. Will Uncle Ell die because I lack faith?

Yesterday afternoon the medical consensus was that there is no real hope. Only the respirator is keeping Uncle Ell alive; his brain damage is apparently too great.

Last night as I prayed, I felt Jesus almost physically transport me to the Garden of Gethsemane, where He wrestled with accepting the Father's will. How the Spirit communicates to one's heart I don't know, but I heard Christ say to me: "Ruth, I know what it is not to want the Father's will. I, too, asked if there wasn't another way. Sometimes the Father's will does include painful things for His greater purposes, but because I've been there, I know exactly how you feel tonight. I'm sad it has to hurt so much, but I'll pick you up and carry you in My arms."

It was beautiful, that overwhelming presence of Jesus. And the majestic strength of the Saviour is clearly being seen by all who meet Aunt Lois. Every visitor leaves knowing he has touched the Spirit of God in her.

I'd never *choose* to go through the events of this week, but it's been precious to have Jesus so close. And, just as I had prayed on New Year's Eve, I've certainly seen an outpouring of Christian love on us all.

Love,
Ruth

Dear Mom and Dad,

Uncle Ell died this evening. He had been scheduled to lead the men's prayer meeting from seven-thirty to eight-thirty, and while the other men were praying in the church, he literally led them all to the Throne of Grace. As his heart stopped beating, and we knew he was gone, Aunt Lois led those of us who were around his bed in singing the Doxology.

Then we went to Rhoda's room to tell her and spent another hour there with friends, singing hymns and praying. We are grieving deeply, of course, but we can also celebrate Uncle Ell's entrance into the very presence of God, knowing that one day we will meet again.

In the middle of the sadness is a peace I've never known before. I thought at first that perhaps I had never before been in a situation where I needed God's peace so much, but then I remembered the day you left me when I was fourteen, and how it felt as if you had all died. I could have used this peace then.

Maybe there is peace this time because I have never before felt so totally accepted and understood in my grief. It's not just the friends around; there were caring people in my life before. It was what Jesus did the other night—He held me and understood. He acknowledged my pain. He didn't try to talk me out of my hurt. That comforts me deeply, though I still cry. I'm learning about God as the Comforter and binder of broken hearts. These are hard days, but I have never loved Him more.

Love,
Ruth

Dear Mom and Dad,

Uncle Ell was buried today.

Last night a wake was held for him. It's a very healing kind of service, where anyone who wants can get up to say what the person meant to him or her. I was amazed at all the small things people remembered that had made such lasting impressions. It made me realize again how every detail of our lives can have spiritual significance in God's hands.

At the end of the funeral, Aunt Lois made a few remarks to the group and then stood by Uncle Ell's picture and coffin while a soloist sang, "Oh, Jesus, I have promised to serve Thee to the end." I guess you know she's planning to stay in Africa. She says God called her to His service before she was married, and that call has never been revoked.

Several indelible impressions have been made on me this week.

For one thing, just dying isn't particularly a witness for Christ. Everyone dies at some point. But when a life has been well spent for Jesus, that person's death is a pointed reminder to keep pressing on toward the goal of finishing the course God has set before me. None of us knows how much time is left.

Uncle Ell could have gone a different way many times in his life. When his firstborn was brain-damaged, when his kids had to go to boarding school, when he could have made a lot of money by staying in the States to work—all those times he could have quit the job God had given him. But in losing his life for Jesus, he has now found it forever.

It will take a while to absorb all the lessons thrown at me this week. I do have more insight into why you made decisions that at the time were hard for our whole family. God's way is

not always the easy one, but it is the one that lasts. I'm glad
you followed, too.

Love,
Ruth

MARCH, 1977

Dear Mom and Dad,

Rhoda is home with her casts on, and Aunt Lois is caring
for her. I don't know how or when—or if—things go back to
normal after something like this, but at least things are going
on. So far there's no real understanding of the "why." Yesterday
Aunt Lois said, "Many have tried to justify God's allowing this
accident to happen, for this or that good reason. But none of
those reasons satisfies me, for none is worth the loss of my
husband. Only one thing satisfies my heart, and that is the
fact that somehow God allowed it for *His* glory. If I never know
why until I get to heaven, that reason alone is enough."

In spite of all the separations our family has gone through,
I realize what a heritage of faith God has given me. And I
mean faith in action when it counts.

Love,
Ruth

For a life previously relatively free of major tragedies,
it seemed we were suddenly being bombarded. Every
letter from home contained bad news. My brother's baby
daughter suffered a spinal cord injury during birth and
would probably be paralyzed all her life. The van carrying
all the household appliances of Dave's sister, Marge,
burned to ashes during her move to Florida. Dave's
brother, Phil, had a fire in his room at college from a
short-circuit in his electric blanket.

Things were no calmer with us. We were robbed again. Dave's schedule was awful; he was so exhausted he could hardly go on. An English baby with meningitis kept him busy day and night, and some Indian friends came frequently with their very sick child. One doctor was on furlough.

I had never seen Dave so physically and emotionally beaten before, not even during his internship, and it scared me. I was used to his being my rock through all my ups and downs. Though my depressions were hard on him, and he often couldn't understand the "why" of them, he accepted them and continued to love me. Now I wasn't sure he'd have the energy to help carry my load, when his own was getting so heavy.

I watched the waves crashing on the beach in front of our house, and felt as though I were down there with them. One wave would throw me down, and just when I got the sand cleaned out of my eyes, another one came from a different direction and I was back down again, eating more sand. I couldn't stand up long enough to run to safety; I could only try to catch a breath in between to survive until the tide would go out and give me a chance.

One verse that helped a lot was Job 23:10: "When he hath tried me, I shall come forth as gold." I held on to the promise that somehow God was using all these hard things to make me a little more golden . . . but most days I wished He'd settle for silver or just some copper.

APRIL, 1977

Dear Mom and Dad,

It was good to have you stop through here on your way back to Nigeria. I'm sure Aunt Lois was glad to have her sister here, and I was glad to have my parents.

Thanks, too, for the book you brought me. I never thought you were too much for psychology books, but it let me know you've been hearing some of my feeble attempts to tell you what I've been struggling with these last few years. The fact that you haven't given up on me has been crucial.

I'm sure it hasn't been easy for you, but not once have you acted as if I were terrible to be struggling, even though I'm not sure you've known exactly what I was struggling about. I haven't been able to totally define it either; that's part of the problem.

Love,
Ruth

Dear Mom and Dad,

Both the Indian and English babies died this week. Not only did their funerals bring us grief for our friends and very raw memories of burying Uncle Ell, but they seemed to symbolize my whole, glorious mission career to this point. Failure.

Yesterday I hit rock bottom. I couldn't even get out of bed to face the day. I lay there all day and thought about my hopes and dreams for life, versus where I am. We were so sure God was bringing us to Africa. He brought all our support in so we could be in Liberia six weeks after candidate school. But what am I doing now? Nothing.

I had a far more spiritual ministry in Portsmouth than I have here. Since we arrived, I've barely been able to keep the family going with all the interruptions of kids coming to my door wanting drinks of water, needing a cup of rice, or just wanting to sit a while. All my nurse's training has gone for nothing. The verses about binding up and healing others only mock me now—I realize they are actually prophecies of Christ, and I was a fool to think they applied to me. It's bad enough to be a failure, but think of all the money people have wasted to send us here, if I'm not doing anything. What am I supposed to tell them?

My thoughts went round and round like this all day, and finally I asked God where I'd gone wrong. I've always been so sure I was following Him, and it had come to nothing.

Then God reminded me of all the miracles He worked to get us to Africa. It wasn't a mistake that I was here.

"Well, if it wasn't a mistake," I demanded, "why is everything so upside down?"

"Ruth, did you come to do My will or yours?"

"What kind of a question is that, God? I wouldn't come all the way to Africa just to do my will."

"Wouldn't you? What is My will for you here?"

"What do you mean, Lord? I'm a nurse. I've been a Bible study leader. I like the nationals. You haven't given me anything to do here."

"Ruth, do you think you might be presuming what My will for you involves? Have you checked with Me, or just headed off with your plans to be the world's greatest missionary?"

I had to admit I had come with a lot of ideas of how to be great. I had a lot to offer God—I was culturally adaptable, I had grown up in Africa, I was friendly to Liberians. I would do everything right that was done wrong when I was a kid. Missionary life would be a breeze.

God showed me something that hurt: it's very possible to want to be a great missionary not for His sake, but for my own. I think I have a lot of listening to do.

Love,
Ruth

Dear Mom and Dad,

Today a song kept going through my head; it's about a person who feels sorry for himself because he's worked so hard for Jesus and gotten no attention. Then Jesus answers and reminds him of all He's done for him.

In the second verse, the singer repents and tells God how eager he is to do whatever big and noble things God requires of him. Then Jesus answers, in effect, "If I give you a cup of water, then all I ask for is a cup of water."

That line arrested my attention. "God, you couldn't possibly have sent me all the way to Africa just to pass out water to those kids at my door every day, could you?"

"And what if I have?"

"But, Lord, that's nothing. I'm ready to do so much more."

"Would you pass out water?"

"But, Lord, there's nothing spiritual about that. I can't even speak their dialect to tell them about You."

"Would you pass out water, Ruth?"

"But, Lord, how can I explain it to my supporters? 'What do you do in Africa?' 'Pass out water.' 'Oh. I see.' It will never work, Lord. They expect a lot more for their money."

"Yes or no."

"Why?"

"Inasmuch as ye have done it to the least of these My brethren, ye have done it unto Me. Will you do it as if it were Me?"

"Okay, Lord. But I don't think anyone else will understand."

So that's my assignment. It does seem awfully small. You never knew I'd have such a smashing career, did you?

Love,
Ruth

JUNE, 1977

Dear Mom and Dad,

I'm muddling along, passing out water and rice, not seeing any wonderful spiritual breakthroughs. At least now I know that it's okay to be ordinary, if that's God's will.

God pinpointed another one of my problems while I was reading Romans 12:1, 2. In the Phillips translation it says, "Don't let the world around you squeeze you into its own mold, but let Him renew your minds from within. Then you will prove in practice what is His good and perfect and acceptable will."

I saw again that my sense of failure stems from trying to live up to my own idealized image of what I should be as a missionary. I also want to be what I *think* others think I should be, including you. I've been squeezed by a whole world of images.

But God is saying that if I do exactly what He says, even if it's just passing out cold water, in time He will prove to me that it is His good, perfect, and acceptable will. I don't have to strive for the acceptance of others.

Another missionary asked me to start a Bible study for the wives on our station. The first week I shared these thoughts about images and molds, and we had good fellowship together. I'll wait to see what God can make of a little bit of water and a missionary Bible study!

Love,
Ruth

What a year. We kept getting robbed, though never as bad as the first time. Once we lost a bike, and another time someone emptied my closet again while we were in the back of the house.

The wife of one of Dave's friends in the States died in a car accident after only a month of marriage.

A good Liberian friend died in January, leaving six children orphaned (his wife had died last year).

The leader of the Medical Group Mission project here went into kidney failure and had to be sent home.

JANUARY, 1978

Dear Mom and Dad,

A friend from Portsmouth sent a tape from the last mission conference, in which a speaker talked about God's principles for missions. He used the verse, "They who sow in tears will doubtless come again with rejoicing, bringing their sheaves with them." So far I've just seen the tears. I trust there will be plenty of rejoicing some day.

I'm so glad we'll be on furlough together this summer. I still have a lot to sort out from my first term, and I know you'll listen. Much of the anger from the past is gone. I'm not nearly as anxious as before. Even when I begin to consider all sorts of terrible possibilities for the future, I realize most things I worry about never happen. For those that do, God has been sufficient in the time of the trouble. I can't borrow His grace ahead. I've just learned to know it will be there when I need it.

I think I've grown enough to not only love you as parents, but to appreciate you as people, too. See you in a few months.

Love,
Ruth

MARCH, 1978

Dave brought me a radio message from the mission: "Charles Frame flying to States for medical care. Loss of peripheral vision and right-sided weakness . . ."

Dear Dad,

You can't have any of all the horrible things I'm imagining, can you? Not now, when I'm finally so ready to see you. Since I'm so used to your absence, I've sometimes wondered if it would matter a whole lot to me if something bad happened to either of you. Twenty years away from each other is a long time, after all. But it does matter, unbearably so. And according to the radio message, you're traveling today, so I can't even call to find out what's happening.

I'm struggling, too, with the old problem of duty versus desire. I've been critical of missionaries who rush home every time there's a family crisis. I thought they must not be very "dedicated." But here I am, wanting to hop the next plane. Maybe it's another sign of my failure as a missionary that I want so much to come, but I feel I'll explode if I have to stay here. I think I'm afraid it will be God's will for me not to go, just so I can learn one more lesson about releasing everything to Him. Intellectually I know that's a pretty lousy concept of God, but it is my feeling.

After church today I lay on the floor and cried my heart out. Why this? Why now? I'm so tired of struggles.

Love,
Ruth

Dear Mom and Dad,

We're coming home! I guess God knew I wasn't in a position to just say I needed to do it and come, so He gave us a "mission reason." There are some short-term doctors here now, but there will be a shortage in the summer. If we go now, we can be back in time to help out then.

Once more, I'm needing help from other people. Many have been here helping me pack up the house, look after the kids, make travel arrangements. God has taken this self-sufficient missionary kid through one situation after another where I've had no choice but to accept help I can't directly return. He's forcing me to see how the Body can show its love for fellow members. And through them, He shows His own love.

We'll be there the day before your birthday, Dad. I'm praying your tests are come out better than expected.

Love,
Ruth

15

ANOTHER GOOD-BYE

MARCH, 1978

Dear God,

I'm here with Dad now, but how can I bear it? He couldn't even see me when I came into his room until I stood exactly in front of him. When he eats, he can't get his fork under the food properly or up to his mouth without dropping it.

He's my *dad*. He's always been so strong, able to take the family through any unexpected happenings. Now he needs our help just to get out of bed. He says one of his big regrets is that his grandchildren will only remember Grandpa Frame as an old man who slobbered his food.

God, help us not to let that happen. May we make sure they also know about a man who loved God above all else, who taught his children not just in formal times, but in the everyday places of life. A man with an overwhelming sense of fairness, not dependent on race or culture. And a grandpa who loved them.

I pray when they do the biopsy on the two lesions they've found on Dad's brain, it will prove to be something treatable. I know the doctors don't expect it to be, but please, God, do a miracle for us.

                                          Love,
                                          Ruth Ellen

Dear God,

I'm glad the hospital let us use the lounge for Dad's sixtieth birthday party. It was nice to see everyone again, but beneath the smiles and candles was the ever-present reality that this could be Dad's last birthday.

I feel a strange numbness inside while I wait to find out what's wrong with him. I haven't called any friends or supporters to tell them I'm home. For once in my life I want to shut out service, duty, missions, people—and just concentrate on family.

You understand, don't you, God?

                                          Love,
                                          Ruth Ellen

Dear Dad,

When they said you had a one in twenty chance of dying during the brain biopsy, it was awful. It was unbearable to see you lying in bed talking with us, and know it might be the last time. Thanks for sharing your struggle with it, too. When you said you couldn't sleep for a while last night, I appreciated your honesty. It's not easy for you, either, even if it is somehow God's will.

But when they rolled you off on the operating room cart, and we watched with tears in our eyes, you said, "Don't forget that Romans 8:28 is still in the Book." I needed that reminder.

Somehow God will work everything together for good. I just can't see how.

Love,
Ruth Ellen

I suppose I wasn't surprised when the surgeon said the biopsy showed two sites of malignancy that were highly resistant to treatment. It was good to cry together, though I kept thinking we should probably be braver. But it was sad to know that time was so short.

It was also good to call for help from the family. This time Chuck was only a phone call and a train ride away, and his visit was a great comfort. He just seemed to know what to do and say that was helpful. Since his daughter Melissa's birth, when they hadn't known if, or for how long, she would survive, they had claimed the verse, "This is the day that the Lord has made. Let us rejoice and be glad in it." They realized that every day is a gift from God, and if they spent their time worrying about tomorrow, they would lose all that God was giving in the present.

Dear God,

We have no idea how long, or short, Dad's time will be, but we will lose it all if we do anything but enjoy each day of his company that we are still given. I wish I'd realized that years ago, when we faced all those separations. Maybe it would have kept me from withdrawing into sullenness before they left. I know it will be hard not to withdraw from Dad now. Please, God, don't let me waste the last chance I have.

Love,
Ruth Ellen

Dear God,

Thank You for these precious times with Dad. It's been wonderful to tell him of some of my struggles in adjusting to mission life and have him understand. He's even agreed with some of the things I've seen as wrong—I realize where I got my sense of fairness!

I'm so glad he could still listen and hear me. I needed his understanding, love, and acceptance. Do I have to lose him, just when I'm getting to know him again?

Love,
Ruth Ellen

Dear God,

It's good to be able to talk about plans for Alice's wedding. Instead of leaving her in a quandary, Dad has told her not to change any plans, no matter what happens to him. Thanks for a Christian family that is able to deal openly with the prospect of coming death, instead of playing the games I've seen so many play.

Dad said when he first realized he would probably die before retirement, he objected and asked You, "But, God, what about my stamp collection and all the gardening I was planning to do?" And You answered, "Charlie, what are stamps and gardening compared to the glories of heaven?"

I've always been afraid of death, but through these days Dad is giving me his last gift as my father. He's taught me a lot about how to live—now he's teaching me how to die.

Love,
Ruth Ellen

APRIL, 1978

The doctor let Dad come home for Easter. It was a wonderful day, with all six of us kids plus the grandchildren here.

I suppose some would find it too painful to have the end drag out like this, but I could do nothing except rejoice that God was giving us these last days to savor as a family. We had been apart a lot, but God kept our love strong.

When we gathered to sing together after dinner, I remembered sitting by Dad in church during our Kano days. He used to tell me how this hymn comforted Grandma Frame during the years she and Grandpa were separated by their mission commitment, and I've claimed it for myself during all our separations:

> *Peace, perfect peace*
> *With loved ones far away?*
> *In Jesus' keeping we are safe*
> *And they.*

This time another verse struck me.

> *Peace, perfect peace*
> *Death shadowing us and ours?*
> *Jesus has vanquished death*
> *And all its powers.*

What a precious gift to have a family that could still sing together, even as death loomed over us.

Dear Mom and Dad,

It was hard to decide to go to Virginia for Tabernacle Church's mission conference. But since you're home now, Dad, and seem to be stabilized, it seemed okay.

We're so glad we went. It's an incredible church. I don't know if they're trying to make up for the "Alabaster Box" sermon or what, but we seem to be wrapped in love here! Since they weren't expecting us this year, we didn't have much to do, but it was so healing to sit under the deep ministry of God's Word and again be reminded of what all the struggles are for. I guess you could say we feel renewed in our "call."

At the ladies' luncheon, all the missionary ladies were to give a few words of testimony or sharing where they were, what they did, etc. They left me until last. I don't know if it was because of remembering the sermon two years ago, or just knowing this isn't an easy furlough for me, but when they announced my name, the women started applauding! I was so overwhelmed, I started to cry, and I didn't stop the whole time I tried to talk. What a way to start my deputation career! I don't know what I said; I just I mumbled a few words about how serving Jesus so far hadn't been very easy for me, and that I'd learned a lot more than I had done. I asked them to please pray hard for me.

Afterwards they came and gave me big hugs and they're still supporting us. I don't understand it, but I sure appreciate it! They accept me without any missionary mask at all.

Love,
Ruth Ellen

Dear God,

When I came home and Dad's color was so blue, I thought he would go at any moment. It was so good of You to allow all six of us kids and Dad's brother and sisters to be there with him.

I guess You know better than I do if unconscious people can hear, even when they can't respond. But in any case, thanks for a family that could sing encouragement to one another as well as trying to offer Dad encouragement in his dying hours. What a great joy it was, as we sang "Great Is Thy Faithfulness," to suddenly hear this very off-key voice joining us for the chorus. There was Dad, eyes still closed, singing with us! It felt like a moment of resurrection!

What a time You gave us. It was so sweet to hear Dad, even from his extreme weakness, speaking of special things and times he remembered. It was a bit as I've always pictured Jacob, when he called his sons to his deathbed to bless them. Even though Dad lapsed in and out of consciousness the rest of the night, the memory of those moments can never be taken away.

Thanks, too, for the privilege of caring for Dad at home during these last days.

Love,
Ruth Ellen

JUNE, 1978

Dear Dad,

Alice is getting married Saturday. I'm going back to Africa next week. I wish we could still talk together, but you haven't spoken for the last two weeks.

As the tension in me mounts, I feel myself doing the very withdrawing I said I wouldn't do. It's hard to go into your room—after all, you don't seem to know if we're there or not. I have lots of packing to do, and there are wedding plans to carry out.

But I'm so glad I caught myself and went to spend time with you once more this afternoon. I didn't think you knew I was there, but when I said, "Dad, I'm glad I came while you could still talk to me," I was shocked to see you trying to respond. It seemed to take every last ounce of energy you had, but you finally got the words out.

"Yes, I'm glad you came while there was still time. I'm glad you came."

Dad, I can't tell you this side of heaven what that meant to me. Maybe you'll know when you get there. It was as if God gave me back the moments I missed with you on my wedding day. I love you.

Love,
Ruth Ellen

Dear Mom,

At Alice's rehearsal dinner tonight, I thought I'd explode. It was so hard to see her fiancee's parents both there and to see you by yourself, and realize that Dad might be dead before the wedding. And then to know I have to go to Africa in five days—it was too much. I sat at the end of the table, unable to eat or be sociable, and cried the whole time. I can't imagine how we'll pull this wedding off tomorrow, if the rehearsal was so hard.

When I came home tonight, I ran upstairs to find a room alone. I guess I hoped Dave would look for me, but I couldn't even let him know how bad I was feeling. It's still very difficult for me to admit my need of comfort to another person, especially to you two or Dave.

I must have cried for an hour, going through all the reasons it was okay for me to go back to Liberia, including God's call and the fact that all five of my brothers and sisters are here to help you. But at the end I had to face a new and startling fact. I needed to stay for *me,* not for anyone else or for how useful I could be. For *my* sake, I need to be here—and my needs are as important as those of anyone else God sends me to minister to!

That decision lifted the heavy load that was crushing me. I found Dave and told him maybe he'd have to go back without me. I needed to wait until this was over before I could return. When he was understanding and didn't judge me for being weak, I realized I'm learning something God started teaching me back in St. Louis: I still expect more from myself by way of duty and service than I do of anyone else. It's even more than God is asking.

Love,
Ruth Ellen

Dear Mom,

I'm glad Dad lived until after the wedding, even if it was only two more days. Some say dying people will wait for "unfinished business"; maybe he was holding on until then.

I'm sorry for you to have lost him, when you've always been so close. But I've seen with both you and Aunt Lois that your grief is not filled with all the regrets of "if only." You lived your lives out well with your husbands.

Thanks for letting me cry the other night when I told you it was too hard to go back. And thanks for crying with me.

Love,
Ruth Ellen

16

LIBERIA AGAIN

JULY, 1978

Dear Mom,

We landed back in Liberia only a week behind schedule. They have some new short-term doctors, so all's well here.

I'm still feeling drained after all the heavy emotional experiences. At the same time, I can also say I have peace. It's been like being closed up in a cabin during a storm—every flash of lightning and crack of thunder seems as if it will destroy you, but then you keep living to see another and another. When it is all over, the quiet at the end is amazing by its very contrast. And only in that quiet are you fully aware of the tension that was in you before. I'm cautiously putting my head out the door to look at the new term. Might it truly be a little less violent?

Love,
Ruth

Dear Mom,

Looks as if this term is going to be as bad as last. Here we are, only back three weeks, and we've been robbed again! I had gone with my friend, Ruth Clark, to do some grocery shopping. I bought extra staples, since we'll be a little short of money while we fix this house. (Did I tell you we were slated to change houses? We'll move as soon as some remodeling is done.)

We had another quick errand to do downtown after shopping, and when we returned to our car, all the groceries were gone! Ruth said, "Well, our things are God's. If He chooses to take them, I guess He has the right."

I thought, *That's my line, and I'm sick and tired of it. This is your first time. It's at least my fifth or sixth.* But I didn't say anything out loud. I knew my thoughts were too unspiritual.

When we reached home, Ruth went in to tell her husband what had happened. He said, "Come and see what was left here." Inside the house were four boxes of groceries, far more than we had lost. Some friends of theirs who worked for Voice of America were leaving the country. They'd emptied their pantry into these boxes and left them with the Clarks en route to the airport. Ruth was ecstatic at God's provisions, and kindly divided them with me.

I felt spanked. If I'd done what she had, and accepted the robbery in faith, I'd have had joy and victory, too. Instead I'd been sulking. Now God hadn't even given me time to enjoy the good sulk I felt I so richly deserved.

I'm glad for the food, of course, but I don't feel like praising the Lord. I just don't want to do it this time. I'd rather wallow in my rotten feelings.

                                                            Love,
                                                            Ruth

AUGUST, 1978

Dear Mom,

I'm depressed again. I'm not sure what's causing it, but I don't like it. I like it even less because I thought God had taken me past that part of my life.

I'm coping by immersing myself in the new house. Your non-artistic daughter has never done more wallpapering or detail work before in her life. I don't want to have company over or see anyone much. The house is a great excuse as well as a wonderful place to hide.

Love,
Ruth

NOVEMBER, 1978

Dear Mom,

It's four months now that I've lived under this cloud. I'm functioning, of course, to the outside world, but inside it's a constant weight. I've been praying about it, but nothing changes. It leaves me a most inadequate wife, mother, and missionary.

We had Communion at church today, but I didn't take it. I told God that if He didn't do something before the Communion service next month, then please to let me die. I'm no good to anyone else this way, and I can't stand living with myself.

Love,
Ruth

Dear Mom,

I spent time again today asking God what was the matter with me, and He took me back again to what I learned in Portsmouth: my depression is basically repressed anger. Fine. But what was I mad about this time?

I thought of the separations, but they seem to have lost most of their sting. I thought of you and Dad, but I feel love rather than the anger I felt during St. Louis days. And although Uncle Ell's and Dad's deaths have left me with sorrow, there isn't anger there, as far as I know. So what, or whom, was I mad about now?

The answer came: "You're angry at Me, Ruth."

"God, I wouldn't dream of being angry at You. You're God."

"But you are angry at Me."

"God, my life depends on You. How could I be angry with you?"

"Accept it. You are."

"But I know You'd never do something purposefully mean to me. I know all the Bible verses about how great You are. I wouldn't dare be mad at You. I love you."

"You can love someone and still be angry at him. What you know and what you feel are often very different. Your depression is from trying to get your feelings in line with your mind without admitting what those feelings are."

God forced me to acknowledge the truth of what He was saying. All these years my anger has been focused on specific things like separations or you. But the actual fact is that I've been furious with God. After all, why did we have to separate? For Him. Who could have stopped all these bad things from happening to me these last two years? He could have. When I finally acknowledged this, I expected to be struck down from Heaven. Who am I to question God?

"Ruth, I know this idea shocks you, but I'm not shocked. I've known your anger was there all these years, even though you didn't recognize it."

I couldn't believe God wasn't furious with me—He was even big enough to handle my anger! This gave me courage to explore a little more inside, and I realized that this particular depression had been with me since the day I got robbed. The groceries weren't such a big deal, and besides, God replaced them. But I remembered that my true feelings that day were, "Why don't

You leave me alone? Ever since I came to Liberia to serve you,
You've done nothing but bad things to me. I'm sick and tired
of it."

Those weren't very acceptable thoughts, even to me, so I
pushed them down. But inside, I was still mad. I never "forgave
God" for all those events. It was like the first time I saw what
an angry person I was, only this time I saw even deeper. As
before, I didn't know what to do, but at least I could acknowledge it. God will have to do the healing.

So I wait. A terrible thorn was exposed today that I didn't
even know was the cause of so much pain.

Love,
Ruth

Dear Mom,

A few days ago, I saw a book on our shelves which I suppose
has been there for several years—*The Release of the Spirit* by
Watchman Nee. As I read it, I knew it was God's answer.

Mr. Nee says we pray for God to use us, yet there's so much
debris in our lives that God must first prepare us. He needs to
get rid of all that stands in the way of our being what we long
to be, fully usable by Him. These obstacles are things we don't
even realize exist such as pride, security in our professions,
anger, and on and on. Since these are part of the external
man rather than the spiritual man, God uses external circumstances to do the pruning.

Nee warns that no one can shorten this process of God's
loving work, but we can lengthen it by resisting and arguing
with every circumstance God allows in our lives. People who
never yield to God's teaching through circumstances become
very bitter people indeed.

The book was most helpful because it didn't gloss over the
fact that the work of God sometimes hurts. Somewhere I picked
up the idea that if I was feeling anything but glowing joy and
excitement, my Christianity was a failure. But now I see so
many other aspects of the faith. Not only does the seed have to

die before fruit can be born, but the glory of Christ's resurrection followed the agony of His death. I've been, and still
am, in a necessary process with God. It's productive, but not
painless.

I think of all God has taught me these last few years. It's
true that I never seemed to learn the lessons in the quiet places.
If I had, I suppose some of these situations wouldn't have had
to occur. But then, I don't know if I could have ever known
God in the same way if I hadn't been forced to cling to Him
so closely. I only know He promises that everything can still
work together for the good of conforming me to the image of
Jesus Christ.

These hard experiences are like final exams. We study like
mad to know God better; but until the test, we don't know
for sure how much we actually understand.

Love,
Ruth

MAY, 1979

Dear Mom,

The more I've thought about this anger at God, the more
I've seen its implications for others as well as for myself. I
realize that I've been bumping into other depressed Christians
for a long time. We even have some on the mission field. When
I listen to each one talk, a situation is usually blamed. "If my
husband just spent more time with me and the kids." "If we
just got more recognition for what we do." "If I were married."
"If Africa weren't so far from home." If, if, if—the illusion
that if whatever it is would change, then "I wouldn't be
depressed."

I believe many Christians besides me are also mad at God.
Maybe it's as hard for them to admit it as it was for me. When
we're angry at any situation (including small inconveniences),
and we believe in the sovereignty of God, then we're actually

mad at Him. He could have changed any of those things, but He didn't. But as "good" Christians, we can't bear to admit that feeling, so we bury it. Then we get depressed and blame anything, and everything, around us.

We hide our true feelings from ourselves and each other. We almost think we can hide them from God! But God is big enough to accept any feeling, no matter how "bad" or unjustified. In confession and forgiveness we can have healing.

Love,
Ruth

JULY, 1979

Dear Mom,

We've been back in Liberia for a year already. In spite of the trauma in the first few months, it's been pretty good.

God still hasn't given me a "great work." Kids continue to come to the door for water. A lot of single missionaries and medical students here for short-term experience drop by for cups of coffee and companionship. It's been fun to try and pass on to them some of the positive encouragement we have received from others.

I see God also using my lonely times in St. Louis. Because I realize how important Linda's open home was to me, it gives me delight to share ours. Each time I open my home to someone in need, her ministry is multiplied. I guess that's how God's Kingdom grows.

One of the greatest surprises has been seeing how God has given me personal fulfillment in spite of Dave's busy schedule. While Dave continues to be gone long hours, God has used that time for serving others. Doing this meets my needs of friendship, too. The speaker in Virginia was right when he said that God will take the very thing you think you can't possibly give to Him and make it the same thing that brings great blessing.

I also remember what Dad said before we came: "Ruth, you'll do a whole lot of seed planting. Sometimes it may look as though none of these seeds are growing, but keep planting. When you look back, you'll see some trees. You just never know while you're planting which seeds God has chosen to grow into trees."

Somehow all these things have made it fun to do the ordinary and believe God will make them into the extraordinary as He sees fit.

Love,
Ruth

FEBRUARY, 1980

Dear Mom,

Just when I think I'm finally getting spiritual and organized, something else comes along.

The house we have now is the first one I've been able to call my own for an indefinite amount of time—my first "personalized" home. It is really pretty, with all the work I did in it during my depression.

Now Dave has the feeling that God may be calling him to change course a bit. The mission has let him teach in the government medical school in the mornings; then he works in the mission hospital in the afternoons and night. He feels for our next term, he should be concentrating more on one thing rather than going in so many different directions. He's thought of going with the government full-time, yet we don't want to leave the mission; we still feel God has called us to be part of their team. Dave's very interested in doing village health work, as most of the pediatric problems he sees could have been prevented in the first place. Another option is to work full-time at the mission hospital, but that wouldn't involve the teaching he loves.

The upshot is that all choices but the mission hospital mean we'll move. It seems unbearable after I've just gotten so settled.

At the same time, I remember Dad's advice that I should never be afraid to plant fruit trees that I might not be around to eat from. Someone else will receive them as a gift from the Lord.

The worst option for me is the village health one. I've never liked "the bush" since I was a kid. I can't imagine living with kerosene refrigerators; they always seem to be exploding in someone's face. And the hardest question is, what would we do with our kids?

Love,
Ruth

MARCH, 1980

Dear Mom,

Dave and I have been at a continuing medical education conference for missionary doctors in Kenya. It's been a fantastic time of fellowship and challenge—we never realized what an army of people there are doing the same kind of work we are.

Unfortunately for me, everyone is talking about village health work, and Dave is growing more and more excited about the idea. Though teaching is his first love, he still doesn't feel he should leave the mission to go with government alone. With village health, there would be a whole different type of teaching, training people how to prevent the diseases that kill so many of them.

I sat and fought inside all through one session. Even after being raised in Africa, I feel I'm a city girl. But worse than the question of "going to the bush" is the other one: how could I ever send my children away to school?

I've always felt God knew that I couldn't bear the separations on both ends of my life and, therefore, has kindly allowed us to live on a station where the girls could walk to a fine mission school. But now this. *Would* God ask me to send my girls away? I have to accept His promise not to give me more than I can bear. If He wants us to go "up-country," then His grace will have to come in that moment.

Love,
Ruth

Dear Mom,
Our women's Bible study this week was from Luke 14. There they were again, those foreboding verses from years ago: "If any man come to me, and hate not his father, and mother, and wife, and children, and brethren, and sisters, yea, and his own life also, he cannot be my disciple."

My children, Lord. Are You really more important than my children?

"And his own life also." My life, Lord? The comforts I think I can't do without in the bush. Are You really more important then those?

The chapter continues to talk about counting the cost of a project before you start. How foolish to build a building halfway and never finish. I felt trapped. I've already started. God has called me to His very best feast, offering all the blessings He promises to those who follow Him completely. Am I going to make my excuses? Am I going to say I've changed my mind and other things are now more important? Will I stop in the middle?

I know that I do want to finish. May God help me accept whatever that includes.

Love,
Ruth

APRIL, 1980

Dear Mom,
Yesterday morning the phone rang at six forty-five. It was my jogging partner. *Good grief,* I thought, *not on Saturday!*

Louisa said, "Ruth, in case you were planning to jog, I thought I should tell you not to. There are lots of soldiers all around. It seems there might have been a coup."

I was awake in an instant. That noise I was half-hearing in my sleep was actually machine gun fire!

I've never presumed to be the heroic type. People like Corrie Ten Boom and Helen Roseveare were made out of different stuff from old chickenhearted me. But there they were—real live machine guns!

We turned on the radio, but both stations were off the air. Oh, for a little American on-the-spot reporting! What was going on? Who was after whom? There was nothing to do but wait. Dave decided to go up to the hospital to see if they needed extra help. Since we live on the opposite end of the compound, I didn't think that was a great idea. I asked him to call when he got there safely.

While I waited for his call, I had lots of time to think. What would I do if that machine gun turned up at my front door, with just me and my three little girls present? What if David was already shot down somewhere?

When I realized that the verses I'd been studying weren't only for the bush, after all. Could I trust God right now with my kids? with my "very life, also"? There was no way to plan what to do if soldiers came to the door, but could I, would I trust God for grace even at that moment, should they come?

I saw what you must have seen years and years ago: our children, our lives, are given by God. Either He's trustworthy to take care of them, no matter what, or He's not.

While we waited, I did experience peace deep in my soul. But I have to confess something—my flesh had a bad headache all day!

Love,
Ruth

AUGUST, 1980

Dear Mom,

Things have remained quite calm since the coup, and life goes on as usual.

You won't believe Dave's new assignment for next term. Our director came from general council meetings to say the mission has a new policy: they will let full-time missionaries work in government positions as their mission assignment! Now Dave can go to the government hospital and medical school full-time when we come back from our furlough.

That means we'll move to a house provided in town, but the girls can be driven to school each morning. Losing the house I love is very small compared to that blessing.

It will be good to see you soon and have a longer furlough. We've decided on Chicago as our home base because Sheri, Rachel, and Stephanie have never lived there. We feel they need a sense of roots.

I'm glad the mission has assigned you to the home office since Dad died. New Jersey will be only a phone call away, instead of an ocean!

                                        Love,
                                        Ruth

17

REST AND RECUPERATION

DECEMBER, 1980

Dear Mom,

This is an extra good furlough. It's great to be here for the normal part of life, the daily ins and outs. Each visit isn't so intense, because it's not the one and only.

We enjoyed being at Dave's brother's wedding.

It's been good to be able to call Chuck and Doreen often during this period that Melissa has been hospitalized again.

It's great to go to lunch with Tom and to talk to you, Mae Beth, and Alice by phone.

Only Marj in Nigeria is inaccessible, but she'll be home before we leave again.

One of the best things is being close to Dave's family. I've always loved them, but with my feelings toward my own family more resolved, I no longer have the feeling of divided loyalty. I can love both sides, with neither the loser. Somewhere that old jealousy that my girls won't know our family as well as Dave's is gone. It doesn't matter anymore; there's enough love to go around. Love seems to grow when you don't try so hard to protect it.

Yes, it's a good year. A happy year. A restoring year. I'm glad God puts some of those in, too!

Love,
Ruth

MARCH, 1981

Dear Mom,

We left the girls with Mom Van Reken in Chicago while we went once again to the missions conference at Tabernacle Church in Virginia. On the way home, we visited various friends and supporters.

When we arrived at Jim and Kathy Ohlson's house about nine o'clock one night, Jim greeted us with the news that Stephanie had fallen off the gym set during recess and broken her arm.

I felt bad, of course, but a broken arm isn't the end of the world. We called home to see how everything was, and Rachel and Sheri said Grandma was at the hospital with Stephanie. Why would they still be at the hospital, if the accident had happened in the afternoon?

It turned out Stephanie was scheduled for surgery the next morning. She'd landed on her elbow and chipped off a piece that had to be wired back.

I couldn't believe my little girl was going to have surgery without me there! I tried to figure out how I could get there by seven in the morning, but there were no flights available. I wanted to start driving immediately, but Dave explained, quite logically, that even if we left immediately, we couldn't make a thousand miles by morning.

I wasn't feeling at all logical and I still wanted to leave at once, but he wouldn't budge. He said that, tired as we were, we would probably have an accident if we drove all night; that Stephanie was in good hands, and that nothing would change if we left now or in the morning.

I knew everything he said was right, but inside everything felt terribly tight. I put my missionary mask back on long enough to call the rest of the people we were scheduled to see in the next few days and explain why we couldn't come. Dave enjoyed playing computer chess with Jim, while I stewed on the couch downstairs. How dare he be so relaxed about it all?

I finally pushed us out of the door by five the next morning. I felt sorry for blowing my missionary image in front of Kathy and Jim, but I couldn't help it.

We got in the car and drove a few blocks, and then Dave asked what on earth was the matter with me. I just started to cry, not even understanding myself what was wrong. But as I cried, memories washed over me of time after time when I had wanted my mommy to put her arms around me and comfort me when I was sick, or hurt, or in trouble, but someone else had always had to do it for her—or no one had done it at all. Now for the same reason—missions—I wasn't there to comfort my little six-year-old the first time she was in a hospital.

Initially I felt anger; God had done it to me again. But as I wept, I realized it wasn't anger I was feeling; it was grief. God had let this happen so I could remember and feel things I didn't even know were still inside of me. His love knew there were more wounds that needed healing. By letting me remember and cry, even two or three decades late, light was coming into the darkness.

I don't share this with you to hurt you. I know you would have been there through the years if you could have. I just need to say there were times in my life that I missed you very much. I love you.

Ruth Ellen

We found Stephanie cheerful with her arm in a cast, enjoying the color TV. Everyone said how brave she'd been, and all was well. She got a little weepy after we arrived, but I'm sure it was a release for her, too.

After a week at home, the doorbell rang, and there stood a lady I'd never seen before, a plate of cookies in her hand.

"Is this Stephanie Van Reken's home?" she asked.

"Yes, it is. May I help you?"

"I'm one of the aides on pediatrics at the hospital. I told Stephanie I'd check on her after she went home."

I invited her in. It turned out that she was the aide who got Stephanie from the emergency room. When she had heard that this little girl's parents were a thousand miles away, she realized how hard that must be for both child and parents, and she began to pray for us. She was off work the day of surgery, so she spent the day at home fasting and praying for our family.

I was amazed at God's precious love for us. He moved a young woman who had never met us before to give herself to us in this ministry of prayer—and He had certainly honored those prayers. Another wonderful lesson in God's trustworthiness with my children.

18

AT HOME AND AT PEACE

JULY, 1981

Dear Mom,

We're enjoying our new Liberian home in town immensely. It's twice as big as the other one—feels like more than a missionary should have.

I still have trouble accepting God's gifts without feeling guilty for them. I realized a while ago that when I worry too much about what He does give, it's the same as worrying about what He doesn't—it's still a focus on things. The apostle Paul says he knows how to be deprived and how to have plenty. Sometimes it's harder to handle the plenty than the little.

Rachel has done a great job of getting us settled in the neighborhood by collecting all the sick-looking babies and bringing them over for care! All three girls speak fluent Liberian English, a big help in this all-Liberian neighborhood.

I'm enjoying living closer to the people of this country. As I see my girls interact with their new Liberian friends, I recall that most of my childhood friends were Nigerian, especially during the nine school months when there were no other missionary kids around to play with.

Maybe we were a help to you, too?

Love,
Ruth

MARCH, 1983

Dear Mom,

This has been a good term. Town living suits me well, and one of the most exciting things it has done is to give me more contact with the international women who also live in town. One woman, who had begun coming to the mission Bible study last year, asked me to teach a new study at her house with some friends who were already getting together.

That group of women has given me more joy than I can tell you. God has blessed their seeking hearts, and all of our lives are changing. I read recently that the cost of ministering to others is that you must first walk through the hard places yourself—you cannot give what you do not have.

For years I thought if people saw my strength they would want to come to Jesus. Now I see that it is when they see His strength in my weakness that they are drawn. How can I share what He's done for me, unless I also share why I needed Him? I could share from my mind, but my heart would still be condemning others' weaknesses as I did before I ever knew the depth of my own needs.

In this group of women, our experiences are not all the same. We've all had some joys; we've all had some sorrows. But when we share with one another who we are, our spirits touch and we share the Christ who is within us. Regardless of our backgrounds, we all need God to heal past pain, restore relationships that are broken or weak, and set us free from the slavery of trying to please others instead of Him.

This group has also given me a renewed appreciation for the blessings of a godly heritage. Left to myself I could have indulged in any sin ever committed on this earth, but I have been saved from many scars because of my early training in God's ways. I believe as well that my multi-cultural upbringing has prepared me to exult in seeing women from so many countries come together for fellowship week by week. A couple weeks ago we had seventeen women present, representing thirteen countries!

I think I have finally come to terms with who I am as a missionary, a missionary kid, and, most importantly, as a person uniquely made by God. I like being me!

Love,
Ruth

SEPTEMBER, 1983

Dear Mom,

This past furlough was another whirlwind. These three-month furloughs are nice, because we get to see you more often, but they do leave me out of breath.

During an evening service at Tabernacle Church this summer, I shared the joy I was feeling in the various tasks God has been giving me to do. Afterward, a lovely older woman came up to me.

"Honey, aren't you the lady who always cries when she talks?" she asked.

I laughed. "Well, yes, I guess I am."

"Well, honey, when I saw you up there tonight, telling how happy you are, I thought, *If God can see that lady through, He can see anyone through!*"

And that's the truth. God is indeed in the business of restoring and healing the bruised and brokenhearted. The traumas of my life may seem small compared to what others have gone through. Nevertheless, they have been real. To know that God can take the very things that Satan wanted to use to destroy me, and use them to teach me more deeply about Himself, myself, and others, is a great miracle. And it gives me confidence to know He can provide that same restoration and healing for others.

Jesus said, "You shall know the truth, and the truth shall make you free." When I no longer have to run and hide from my feelings, but can tell Jesus, as well as others, about them, I'm living in the truth of what and who I am. That frees me to know more of God's truth as well.

There's total freedom in Jesus. A freedom to be God's me!

Love,
Ruth

MARCH, 1984

Dear Mom,

We had an uneventful trip back to Liberia, but guess what's facing me now.

All these years I've assumed Sheri would attend high school at the American Cooperative school in town. Suddenly she and Dave are talking about her going to a mission boarding school in Ivory Coast. All her friends are going there, so she thinks she'd like to go, too.

It's stirred up feelings that I thought were completely healed. With my brain, I've realized that boarding schools could probably be part of God's will for some children—but I've never planned to send mine.

I told Dave and Sheri that this is not something I can decide; it's up to them. I realize that's a cop-out but, in spite of all the healing God has already done in me, I'm still bumping into a wall that I built many years ago. That wall has to go before I can see clearly in this matter, and I don't know how to move it.

Love,
Ruth

APRIL, 1984

Dear Mom,

Today a visitor spoke to our Bible study group about our need to go back and let God heal the painful memories from our past. She put into words what I've seen God doing these past few years. At the end she asked if anyone would like prayer and, though it was a bit embarrassing since I'm leading the group, I realized God was offering me a chance to ask for more of the total healing I so much desire. While I see many places in my life He has already touched, Sheri's decision has shown me that there are still some shadowy spots.

As the women prayed for me, many feelings from the past came back, and as the feelings came I cried. The first feeling was the same one I had when Stephanie broke her arm, that longing for comfort when I felt pain or loneliness. So often no one had been there who knew my need or how to comfort me.

Then I came home and prayed alone. It was as if all the sadness of my life swept over me like a monstrous tidal wave. Why had there been so many, many times when no one was there?

Then Jesus spoke to me again. "Ruth Ellen, I was there, every single time."

"But, Jesus, I never knew it. I wanted someone to hold me. You didn't do that."

"Do you remember how I held you the night before Uncle Ell died? My Presence can be that real. My child, there hasn't been one moment of your life that you've been completely alone. I have loved you with an Everlasting Love, and My arms have never let you go."

When it was over, there was a deep, deep sense of peace. I was drained, but I felt God's love for me in a personal, special way.

Love,
Ruth

"What do I do now, Lord?" was my question. I saw this big hole of hurt that needed to be comforted. I saw that Jesus wanted me to know He had always been there. But something still felt unfinished. As I prayed, I knew I needed to tell my mother.

How could I do it? For so many years I carried all these things in my heart without knowing it. Now I realized how many things I wanted to say but couldn't. Was there any way to go back, or was the past lost forever?

From somewhere deep inside came a compulsion to ask Christ to go back with me to those hidden moments. I needed to feel again what they were like, so that I could understand and write to my mother what I was not yet able to speak aloud.

It wasn't easy to write them. Many times I came close to stopping, because the memories hurt too much. I had to face emotions that had been suppressed for many years.

Writing these letters was only a part of a whole process, not the beginning or the end. As I wrote, I was excited to recognize a clear pattern of God's leading and direction in my life. Even before I knew I needed healing, He was slowly working. He used each situation in His wonderful, redemptive way. I could not have handled the exposure of all my hidden feelings at one time, but God didn't do that. How loving, shaping, and consistent was His hand.

I learned one other thing as well: that He gave me tears to wash away the pain. After years of trying to be brave, particularly of denying the pain of "little Ruthie,"

it was good to cry. Not that it felt good while the tears
were streaming and I was choking on my pain, but after
the tears there was a sense of cleansing.

JUNE, 1984

Dear Mom,
   As I read these letters now, they almost feel like my friends.
I can forgive the little girl I was, for not being all she thought
she was supposed to be. The greatest joy has been to understand
for the first time in my life that God is the "God of all Comfort."
I could not understand that until I recognized how much I
needed His comfort.
   I pray you will receive this as the gift of myself I send
to you, and I hope you can accept me as you find out who I
really am.

                                                   Love,
                                                   Ruth

JULY, 1984

   After receiving all these wonderful revelations about
my need for comfort, I decided to do a study on that
word. First I had to figure out what comfort is. The
dictionary says it is "freedom or relief from pain, and
anything that contributes to that relief." Note that it is
not necessarily the total absence of pain or sorrow, but
relief. In a Bible dictionary it says that comfort means
"to sigh with someone."
   I received a beautiful definition of comfort from a dear
friend who had suffered for years with depression. She
had even been hospitalized and received electric shock
treatments and many, many different programs of medi-
cation. Nothing ever helped for long, until she came to

know the comfort that Jesus could give. This is how she defined comfort.

Comfort is:

1. Not being alone in your suffering.

2. A friend who lets you cry and doesn't say it will be all right.

3. Having someone who is just there with you in times of stress.

4. Having someone see your family's needs and quietly meet them.

5. A friend who prays for you when you can't pray for yourself.

6. A friend who says, "I am there when you need me."

7. Caring in whatever form it takes.

Next I went to Scripture to see what it says about comfort. It is unbelievable how pervasive this idea is throughout Scripture. How had I missed it before?

In Ecclesiastes 4:1-2 I read: "Again I looked and saw all the oppression that was taking place under the sun: I saw the tears of the oppressed—and they have no comforter; power was on the side of their oppressors—and they have no comforter. And I declared that the dead, who had already died, are happier than the living, who are still alive" (NIV). Comfort must be important, if it's better to be dead than comfortless.

In Matthew 5:4 I read that comfort is a blessing: "Blessed are those who mourn, for they shall be comforted." The blessing is not in the mourning, but in the comforting.

And above all else, Scripture says comfort is the ministry of God Himself. In Isaiah 61 I found a beautiful picture of this: "The spirit of the Lord God is upon me; because the Lord hath anointed me to preach good tidings unto the meek; he hath sent me to bind up the brokenhearted, to proclaim liberty to the captives, and the opening of the prison to them that are bound; To proclaim the acceptable year of the Lord, and the day of vengeance of our God; to comfort all that mourn; To

appoint unto them that mourn in Zion, to give unto them
beauty for ashes, the oil of joy for mourning, the garment
of praise for the spirit of heaviness; that they might be
called trees of righteousness, the planting of the Lord,
that he might be glorified" (vv. 1-3).

God comforts not just those physically bound, but
those bound within as well. People can be held captive
not just in a physical sense, but by memories of feelings
they thought they shouldn't have had!

So how does God comfort us? Sometimes it is through
the comfort of His Word. Other times it is with an
experience such as I had when Uncle Ell died, and God
showed me how deeply He cared. Very often, however,
it is by His Holy Spirit working through other people.
In II Corinthians 1:3-4, God tells us this very clearly:
"Blessed be God, even the Father of our Lord Jesus
Christ, the Father of mercies, and the God of all comfort;
Who comforteth us in all our tribulation, that we may
be able to comfort them which are in any trouble, by the
comfort wherewith we ourselves are comforted of God."

There is an important implication here. We can only
share what we have received. If we have never known
God's comfort, how can we share it with another?
Perhaps that is why the ministry of comfort seems to be
such a barren field. In our efforts to be tough, in our
refusals to admit our weaknesses, failures, and hurts,
we have never opened ourselves to this work of God
within. Being empty, we have nothing to give to anyone
else.

I also read through the book of Job. There's a great
picture there of what comfort is not, as portrayed by
Job's friends. The friends did all right the first week,
when they were silent. But when they tried to figure it
out and explain to Job what God must be doing, they
only increased his frustration. They almost forced Job
into rebellion, as their words of explanation and exhorta-
tion pelted him.

By contrast, God gave Job time. He let him vent his feelings and ask his questions. He waited without jumping in. When the pain, frustration, anger, hurt, and questions had all been put forth, God finally answered. And the first thing He did was to condemn Job's friends for giving explanations about a situation they knew nothing about. (How often do we try to explain God's ways when we're also guessing?)

Then God turned to Job. He never did explain the reason for Job's suffering; He only reminded him of who He is. And in God's presence, Job's heart became still again. A God as big as the one who revealed Himself to Job could be trusted totally, even before the "whys" were answered. Job was comforted, and he was restored.

God gave me a whole new vision of how much He really cares for His children, and how He expects us to care for one another.

AUGUST, 1984

Dear Mom,

Today Sheri left Africa. She decided to go live with her Grandma and Grandpa Van Reken and start high school in the States, so she won't have to change when we go on furlough next year. I feel my life has come full circle.

At the airport, there were a few moments when the pain was so intense I had no recourse but to use my old blocking-out techniques. When Sheri went through the doors to the plane, I had the same choking feeling that I had my first night at boarding school. She looked unbelievably grown-up walking out on the tarmac all by herself, turning around to wave good-bye. There was no way I could reach my baby to call her back again.

Coming home from the airport reminded me of coming home from a funeral or like going to Aunt Jennette's house after you left me in high school. Once more, the thing I dreaded had happened; nothing could change it. But the difference was that this time I can acknowledge my grief and loss now, as it is occurring. I knew I could come home and express that grief to Christ, and allow the healing to start *now*, instead of ten years from now.

So today I did what I never thought I could, and only God's healing has made it possible. I suppose every parent has to face this time—the time of trusting and letting go.

Lots and lots of love and thanks, Mom, to both you and Dad.

Love,
Ruth

A FEW MORE WORDS
FROM RUTH

While the need for comfort and healing is universal, and the following principles apply to people of many other backgrounds, I want to address specific issues faced by the Third Culture Kid (TCK)* communities in particular.

There is one common factor in every TCK's experience. It is the repetitive cycle of separation and loss. This includes not only separation from parents but separation from friends as well. If it wasn't my turn to go, it was someone else's. A whole world is lost when a station or country is changed. Non-TCKs face separations too, but in a TCK's world they are constant, beginning early and becoming a way of life. The recognition and handling of the grief these losses produce are critical factors in the child's development.

The grief can be masked in many different ways such as anger, withdrawal, rebellion, compliance, depression, an "I don't care" attitude, or even a joking manner. Very often it is seen in the child's acting "tough" or super-independent. Too often we punish or judge others before discerning the root cause behind the behavior. All who are involved with children need to ask God for special sensitivity.

As Hugh Missildine says in his book, *Your Inner Child of the Past*, whenever there is a prolonged loss of relationship between parent and child, for *whatever* reason, children go through several stages. The early stage is one of profound grief. There is a great deal of crying and longing for the parents' return. This may last for several days or, in some instances, much longer.

Soon the grief turns into despair. This is the second stage. It becomes obvious that Mom and Dad will not be returning. There isn't one thing the child can do to change that situation. He alternates for a period between grief and despair.

After a while, however, the final state of detachment begins. The child no longer seems to care. It's as if he has forgotten about his parents. When they do return, he may act as if he hardly knows them.

Detachment is a major defense mechanism against emotional pain. It happens routinely in short separations as well as longer ones. The first day of summer camp many children want to go home, but by the end of the week they ask to stay longer. This type of detachment is normal. It is part of a healthy maturing process when a child learns to function as his own person. It is also healthy for the child to have the security of home where he can retreat after his foray into the world of independence.

However, if a child is separated physically or emotionally from his parents for a long period, this detachment can reach such an advanced stage that he remains there. He may find it difficult to feel affection toward his parents again.

Some TCKs have ended up in this final stage and have never gotten out. They've had no other defense against the pain. Too often we have mistakenly called it "independence."

The detachment has many forms. It can be something as simple as preferring boarding school to being at home. A child who spends his whole vacation visiting everyone in the village but won't spend time alone with his parents may show detachment rather than good adjustment.

As adults, some TCKs exhibit open hostility toward their parents through a very rebellious lifestyle—many, however, express a feeling of neutrality. "If my folks are here it's fine. If they're not, it doesn't matter. I'm used to it." More effort may be made to see friends from boarding school days than to pick up the phone and call home. Letters may be sporadic if at all. Times of reunion may be so filled with things to do there is no time left to talk.

As Christians we must deal with two basic concerns. The first is how to help those who have already experienced the negative results of excessive grief and loss. The second is how we can minimize these effects in the future.

To begin, we must acknowledge that even separations done for Jesus' sake have repercussions. We have often pretended this isn't so. We want our faith to make us immune to them. Truth comes before healing.

The effects are two-sided. Positively, because I had to cope alone with many different situations, I have a certain confidence. I expect to find a way out of puzzling circumstances. I can enjoy trying new things.

Negatively, this confidence can lead to arrogance. I assume I can handle everything on my own. I think I don't need anyone else. I keep my distance from others. It is easy to refuse the help others would give. This is contradictory to all God teaches about needing to live within the Body Life of His Church.

TCKs have coped with their cycles of separation and loss in many different ways. Some have faced their grief, wept at the good-byes, and stayed in close touch with family and friends. Their lives are positive, healthy, and happy.

Perhaps many are like me, committed to the faith and principles with which I was raised, yet experiencing the struggles I have described. We are coping, productive people, yet inside is that tender core. We presume we are the only ones who feel it. Others have felt hopeless enough to commit suicide. Still others reject the God they feel has been responsible for these losses. Some lash back at their parents and a whole system by living a defiant lifestyle.

There are the parents who rejoice in the emotional health seen in their children. Other parents have wept for years before God, asking for the healing of that injured child or children.

To those who already feel wounded for whatever reason, I promise you this—it is not too late. Jesus *is* the Redeemer and can remove the scars caused by the hurts of years ago. Perhaps you still feel anger and bitterness toward those who hurt you, even though it may have been unintentional, or unrecognized, on their part. Go to Him first, screaming out your feelings if you must. Grieve for the pain you experienced. It's possible to finish the grieving process even years later. Then, when you have finished pouring it out to Him, let Him heal you. By His own Spirit, He will let you know that He understands your anger toward Him. He is not only the Redeemer, He is also the Comforter.

Then may He give you the grace to be reconciled to those who have wounded you—parents, teachers, friends. And may they have the grace to accept your confessions of hurt as a gift of yourself rather than being defensive about them. This book would never have been published if my mother had been defensive. I thank God, however, that when I sent her these letters, she responded in love, sympathy, and understanding. She understood I was not blaming her but simply wanting to share with her who I was. It was an essential part of my healing.

From those of you who feel none of these issues apply to your situation, or you have already experienced any healing needed, I ask love rather than judgment for those who have struggled more. I have been grieved when asked why I don't concentrate on telling about the "ninety-five percent of TCKs who are doing fine." It is as if the other five percent are an embarrassment and should be hidden from sight.

I do not quarrel with the fact that there are a great number of success stories among TCKs. I praise God it is so. But when the Shepherd had ninety-nine sheep safe in His fold, He spent all His energies to go and find the one who was lost. Surely our Great Shepherd would give us His same heart to lovingly seek even one who got lost or hurt along the way.

To parents and TCKs who are still in the separation cycles, I say again it is not necessarily sinful or wrong to ever separate. God leads each of us in our family situations. For me as a child, and now as a mother, I believe His will can involve separations.

It is necessary, however, to allow the grieving process to take its healthy course during these times. Be aware that the anger or withdrawal you see may be your child's way of handling the pain. His obnoxious behavior may be an indication of anxiety or grief.

I remember having a good time on family outings during vacations from school. When I realized how much I was enjoying myself, I'd make a decision to not allow those feelings. As I withdrew into a sullen mood, the affair was destroyed for everyone. I simply refused to allow myself to be happy if it all had to end so soon.

As a parent, recognize your own tendency to withdraw. "Can't wait until the kids go back to school and it's quiet again." Do you really prefer having your children away rather than being with you? Or is it your way of coping with the coming separation too? Be sure you do not communicate that silent thought to your child even through teasing about how nice it is when life is more peaceful in their absence.

Most importantly, when your child does tell you that it's hard for him to go away, don't immediately try to "cheer him up." Acknowledge his feelings. Ask questions to show your concern. Try to discover the underlying anxiety.

Remember that separation anxiety may be hidden behind other expressed fears, rebelliousness and "I-don't-care" attitude, etc. Rather than giving pat answers and assurances, show that you care how the child feels. Leave the door open for communication.

Help your child to accept his feelings without guilt. "I know that leaving is hard, and it's okay to cry about it. Life has these hard moments. Sometimes we have to do what seems right even when it's not easy. But always remember that Jesus understands it isn't easy for you and so do we. It's not easy for us either. Write us when you're happy or sad. We want to hear both. Our love for each other is strong enough that we can love each other even when there are miles between us."

Parents are not the only ones who can help TCKs deal with separations and grief. Understanding teachers, dorm parents, and other adults in the community can help TCKs to accept the validity of their feelings and then find the comfort God promises.

An increasing number of organizations are providing policy changes and flexibility for families to reduce the amount and frequency of separations. Educational options are expanding. Relocations are not as frequent. Finances are more available for TCKs to visit their families during school vacations and for parents to visit their children in school.

These things, together with a healthier grieving process when the inevitable separations do come, will allow ever greater expression of the positive side of the TCK lifestyle. The gifts we have of a large world view, the ability to move between several cultures easily, and the enjoyment of friendships with people of varied backgrounds are all things God can use mightily. Satan wants to hold us back. Jesus wants to set us free.

May we become a model of redemptive, comforting love. We

need it, first for ourselves and then to share with others in this broken, hurting world.

*Third Culture Kid communities include those where children from one culture are raised for a significant period of time in a culture other than their own. These most typically include not only families involved in missionary service, but also those working in the diplomatic corps, military service, and international business.

EPILOGUE

I *'ve seen many Ruth Ellens in my practice as a marriage and
family therapist. Her story isn't just a "missionary problem,"
but is common to many Christians. For all our talk about bearing
one another's burdens, many hurting Christians find themselves
alone and isolated, unable to find other believers who will accept
and love them in spite of the "unacceptability" of their feelings—
unable to find people who will treat them as God does. It is a
sad truth that at times people have found the church to be a place
for looking good rather than a place where struggles are shared
and accepted.*

*Ruth's story is a frank recounting of her growth from a faith
based on what she was taught to one based on what she experienced
firsthand. As I read her story I was inspired, as I have been by
many of my clients, by her courage to challenge the foundations
of her faith—to see what holds up to the test of life's experiences.
Like many before her, Ruth found that God was not fragile, nor
was He waiting for an excuse to pounce like a cat on an unsuspect-
ing mouse. The same God who listened to Job's questioning, to
the psalmist's anguish, to Jonah's vindictiveness, and to Elijah's
depression also met Ruth Ellen Van Reken with His eternal
patience, compassion, and understanding.*

*Letters Never Sent vividly shows us that emotions cannot be
ignored, denied, or repressed without consequences. I have often
marveled at how we Christians can so value the spiritual and
cognitive aspects of our person while devaluing the emotional
aspect—as if God, when He was creating human beings, only
got two-thirds of it right! We must come to appreciate that feelings,
too, were created by God as a tool to bring us into greater honesty
with God, others, and ourselves. Ruth's story illustrates that coming to terms with our honest emotions is an important channel
for spiritual growth.*

*But where do we turn for help with our emotions? We trust
schools to develop our cognitive abilities and churches to encourage
our spiritual maturing, but when it comes to emotions, we're
often stuck. When Ruth turned to God for healing, He brought*

people *into her life to lead her to His truth. There was Linda, the woman in St. Louis who first confronted Ruth with her anger. There were the leaders at the Marriage Encounter weekend, who taught her the validity of her feelings. There was the visitor to her women's Bible study, who spoke about letting God heal painful memories. Although Ruth spent plenty of time alone with God, pouring out her heart, and He was certainly the one who brought about her healing, He continually used other people to nudge her along from step to step.*

As a counselor, I'm aware that there is still a stigma for many Christians to the idea of working with another person on their emotions and relationships. Somehow it is easier to accept that God may use physicians to heal the body, and pastors and missionaries to heal the soul, than it is to accept that God might use counselors or other empathetic Christians to bring healing to our emotions and relationships.

Letters Never Sent is a challenge to all of us to have the courage to be open and vulnerable with our hurts as we struggle to become more fully the community God ordained us to be. As Christ prayed for the Church, "May they be brought to complete unity to let the world know that you sent me and have loved them even as you have loved me" (John 17:23).

DAVID NORTON, PH. D.

David Norton, a marriage and family therapist at Centennial Counseling Center in St. Charles, Illinois, is a graduate of Houghton College, Trinity Evangelical Divinity School, and the University of Wisconsin at Madison.

BIBLIOGRAPHY

1. *"God Moves In a Mysterious Way"* by William Cowper.

2. *"Peace, Perfect Peace"* by Edward H. Bickersteth.

3. The Release of the Spirit. Watchman Nee., Sure Foundation, copyright 1965.

4. Your Inner Child of the Past. Hugh Missildine, M.D., Simon and Schuster, copyright 1963, pp. 245-246.

5. All Scripture quotations are from the King James Version unless otherwise indicated.

ORDER SHEET
FOR

Letters
Never Sent

1 to 2 copies . . . .$7.95 each

3 to 5 copies . . . . .7.50 each

6 to 9 copies . . . . .7.00 each

10 or above . . . . .6.00 each

Please add $2.00 postage and handling for the first book. For each additional book, please add 50 cents more per book through 5 books. For each book over 5 copies, add 25 cents per book.

For overseas surface mail, please add $1.00 to the above total. If airmail is desired, please specify and that amount will be added to the total for the books ordered and sent as a bill.

"Letters" P.O. Box 90084, Indianapolis, IN 46290-0084

Please send _____ copies of <u>Letters Never Sent</u> by Ruth E. Van Reken

Mail to:

Name _____

Address _____

City _____ State _____ Zip _____

Country _____

Number of copies _____ at $_____   Total $_____

Postage for first copy   Total $ 2.00

Postage for up to next 4 at .50 @   Total $_____

Postage for add'l copies at .25 @   Total $_____

                                    Grand Total $_____

Please enclose check or money order in U.S. Dollars. Thank you.

"Letters" P.O. Box 90084, Indianapolis, IN 46290-0084